The Ultimate Rush Hour Recipe Collection

EFFORTLESS ENTERTAINING, FAMILY FAVORITES, ONE-POT WONDERS AND PRESTO PASTA ... ALL IN ONE COOKBOOK!

By Brook Noel

TITLES IN THE
The Rush Hour Cook™ Series:

THE RUSH HOUR COOK™: WEEKLY WONDERS
19 WEEKLY DINNER MENUS COMPLETE WITH SHOPPING LISTS

THE ULTIMATE RUSH HOUR RECIPE COLLECTION: EFFORTLESS ENTERTAINING, FAMILY FAVORITES, ONE-POT WONDERS AND PRESTO PASTA ... ALL IN ONE COOKBOOK!

RUSH HOUR RECIPES: RECIPES, TIPS, AND WISDOM FOR EVERY DAY OF THE YEAR

TO ORDER VISIT YOUR FAVORITE BOOKSELLER OR ORDER ONLINE AT WWW.CHAMPIONPRESS.COM OR
LOG ON TO WWW.RUSHHOURCOOK.COM

Join the free Daily Rush e-mail list for recipes, tips, and trivia delivered free by e-mail Monday through Friday.

Also by Brook Noel...
The Change Your Life Challenge: A 70-Day Life Makeover Program for Women
Learn more at www.changeyourlifechallenge.com

10 9 8 7 6 5 4 3 2 1
ISBN 1-932783-99-7

All rights reserved. No part of this book may be reproduced or transmitted in any form or by any means, electronic or mechanical, including photocopying, recording, or by any information and retrieval system, without permission in writing from the copyright owner.

For multiple sales or group discounts contact Champion Press, Ltd.,
4308 Blueberry Road, Fredonia WI, 53021 www.championpress.com

THE RUSH HOUR COOK

FAMILY FAVORITES
by Brook Noel

THE TALES AND RECIPES OF A CORPORATE WOMAN TACKLING TODAY'S KITCHEN

CHAMPION PRESS LTD.
MILWAUKEE, WISCONSIN

DEDICATION

For my family, who put up with one zillion tasteless dinners, to find the recipes that were worth committing to ink.

Contents

IN THE BEGINNING...
SIDES, SOUPS AND STARTERS

Potato Shapes	16
Sugar Carrots	17
Spastic Salsa	17
Aunt Joan's Popovers	17
Potato Salad in a Pinch	18
Chicken Dumpling Soup	19
Tasty Tortellini Soup	20
Quick Chips	20
Cheesy Scalloped Spuds	21
Marvelous Mushroom Rice	22
Quickslaw	22
Crazy for Couscous	23
Potato and Broccoli Bake	24

A MERRY MIDDLE...
MAIN MEALS IN MINUTES

Tantalizing Taco Salad	26
Parmesan Pasta Bowl	27
Let-me-Soak Chicken	28
Presto Pasta	29
The Other White Meat	30
Soup and Sandwich Stops:	
#1. The Big Dipper	34
#2. Make Mine A Melt	35
#3. The Super-Stack	36
Must-Have Meatloaf	37
Christmas Eve Chili	38
Delightfully Dijon Chicken	40
Sammy's Favorite Noodle Bake	41
Ultra-Quick Chicken and Rice	42
Super Stroganoff Supper	43
Chicken Cordon Blue	44
Turkey-Stuffing Casserole	45
"Pizza Pockets"	46
One Dish Meat and Potatoes	47
Mexi-Casserole	48
Quick Fix Salsa Chicken	48
In-a-Pinch Pork Chops	49

FAMILY FAVORITES

Pizza Bake	49
Fine Fettuccini	50
Shell Stuffer	50
Beef Mix	53
(Includes meatloaf, meatballs & Salisbury steak)	

A Sweet & Happy Ending...

Banana Cream Pie	56
No Bake Scrumptious Chocolate Peanut Butter Squares	56
Skinny Pancakes	57
Gramma Harriett's "Red Hot" Apple Crisp	58
Manic for Maple Butter!	58
Champion Chocolate Cookies	59
Fanciful Fruit Dream	60
Baked Cinnamon Apples	60
You Choose-the-Chip Cookies	61
Chocolate Dipped Strawberry's	61
Cinnamon Streusel Coffee Cake	62
Snicker™ Bar Salad	62

Etcetera...

A Few Things You'll Need to Know	7
The Birth of the Rush Hour Cook	9
The Electronic Supermarket	18
How to Become a Certified Potato-Head	21
Click for Savings	27
Edible Finger-paints	28
Add Some Spice to Your Life	29
Gourmet Tips	30
From the Toolbox of Tips	31
Mail a Meal	34
A Blast from the Past	35
A Must-Have List	36
Tried and True Timesavers	40
Potato Resuscitation 101	44
Useless Turkey Trivia	45
The Art of Bulk Cooking	51
Personal Shopper – List # 1	64
Personal Shopper – List # 2	66
Personal Shopper – List # 3	68

A Few Things You'll Need to Know

Pay close attention when you see this symbol. It means that you are about to uncover a 'Mother-Knows-Best' tip which will save you countless headaches when feeding your children.

While every recipe chosen for The Rush Hour Cook™ can be prepared quickly, the recipes marked with this symbol may very well be faster than a speeding bullet. This clock also denotes time-saving tactics, make-ahead options and the like.

At the end of this book, you'll find a section called, Your Personal Shopper. I've included pre-planned menus and grocery lists to get you through those rough weeks when you don't feel like planning—which is just about every week, for me! These are the recipes that I now use much to my family's satisfaction and success.

Serve It Up—All recipes are sized for 6 Servings, unless otherwise noted. If you have a family of 3 or 4, consider adding a few more members or better yet, make the full recipe anyway. Use the rest for lunches the following day, or freeze these extras as healthy, homemade options to those ready-made, chemical-laden convenience-meals.

High-fat, some-fat, low-fat or no-fat—Most of the recipes within this book are either low in fat or easily adaptable for low fat options. When prepared this way, the caloric and fat intakes coincide with each meal, containing less than 30% fat.

Make Your Misto™—Like most cookbooks, almost every recipe calls for cooking spray. Instead of using the aerosol cans that you can buy in the store, purchase a Misto™ or other non-aerosol pump. With these pumps, you can add a bit of olive, canola or vegetable oil and they will convert the oil to spray. This allows you to use the minimum amount of oil and avoid the nasty-chemicals found in their store-shelved-counterparts.

INTRODUCTION: THE BIRTH OF THE RUSH HOUR COOK

This all started very innocently. I am the owner of a successful, small publishing company, and while talking to a trusted friend and colleague, I realized there was a need for quick dinner solutions with simplistic ingredients and surreal taste. After talking to many home cooks, I realized there was a need for "little books"—not tomes with 401 recipes for sugar cookies and 837 variations of chili. No, what people needed, I discovered, were simple recipes for good food, in a nice, little volume. Busy moms and dads could toss it in their purse, decide what to eat while driving home (or arranging Johnny's soccer schedule), or take it to the grocery store since it would be small enough to double as a shopping list. It didn't take me long to decide that Champion Press™ would publish just such a book.

What wasn't so clear was who would author this new, indispensable guide. Champion has a slew of successful cookbook authors. While trying to decide which writer to assign to the project, a friend of mine suggested that I author the series. Keep in mind that this same friend, when in college, witnessed my attempt to microwave a non-microwaveable pizza, and said nothing when I forgot to remove the plastic wrap. Needles to say, my lack of domesticity has long been evident. (I can't iron anything without creating more wrinkles than I started with; although I think this has to do more with my being left-handed than my actual skill level.) I do not sort laundry by colors, fabrics or labels. And, more than once, I have been spotted purchasing finger Jell-O™ premade at the deli. So I asked her, "Why on earth should I write a cookbook series?"

"Well," she said simply. "Think about it... you are the absolute Queen of Incapable Cooking." (I tried not to glare at her as I listened to this

FAMILY FAVORITES

rationale.) She continued, "In order for you to find 30-50 recipes—you will have to cook 200-300—*at least!* You will have to taste-test more than probably any other cook on the planet! Plus, if *you* can cook something quickly—and have it taste good...well...then...it's fool proof!" she rambled excitedly.

"Huh," I replied.

While I wasn't thrilled with this exchange, I had to admit that her reasoning had merit. Earlier in the week, I had watched my daughter excitedly announce to fellow grocery shoppers that it "must be a holiday!" When another shopper stated that she wasn't aware of any holidays, Sammy quickly explained, "My mom is cooking from a real-live recipe... not a box! It must be a holiday! She has never done that before." I smiled meekly, holding up my canister of marjoram in defense. The other women just snickered and cast condescending stares.

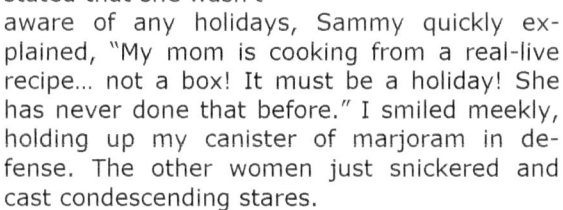

Later that night, I brought the subject up to my husband and mother while I was busy wrapping leftovers in the kitchen. "Mom—did you buy this plastic wrap at the dollar store?" I asked while fighting with the plastic and its supposedly quick-cut-tooth-grabber on the box edge.

"Yes—why?" she asked from the table.

"It doesn't really work so well," I grumbled while yanking yet another yard in attempt to secure my dish. It took about 18 yards and two sailor knots to secure the plastic to the bowl. My husband was entering the kitchen just as I secured the last knot.

"Need some help, honey?"

FAMILY FAVORITES

"I'm fine; it's just the wrap." Of course, he then proceeded to wrap three more dishes with metric precision that didn't waste a millimeter of the dreaded plastic.

"Anyway," I said, returning to the table. "What would you guys think of me writing a cookbook?" My husband made this familiar noise that he makes when he thinks someone is telling a joke, but isn't sure. My mother tried to look engrossed by the television—even though it wasn't turned on. "Well?" I urged.

"Is something wrong with the television?" my mother asked.

"It's not turned on," I said simply.

"I better look at that," Andy said as he rose. Without so much as a backward glance, they both left the table.

In that moment, *The Rush Hour Cook*™ was born.

It hasn't been an easy road, but I'll admit I had ulterior motives for writing this series. I am energetic and frequently work out through the martial arts and running. While my physical endurance is strong, my diet appalls most people (and it actually appalls me as well.) I can live for a week on nothing more than soft pretzels and Twizzlers™. This is not something that makes me proud. My life is a zoo of insanity that allows very little time for cooking let alone making frequent trips to the grocery store. But as an Editor and Publisher, I frequently read about health issues, preservative dangers and other influences our diet has on our body. I wanted to see if I would actually feel better if I found my vitamins in food, instead of the buy-one-get-one-free sale at GNC. I also wanted to minimize my risk of future health ailments. After all, cook or no cook, I am a mom—and I want to be around many,

many years to enjoy my beautiful child and family. I hope that throughout this process I can pass on some healthful knowledge and good habits along the way.

My last motive for authoring this series is to recreate the family dinner in my home. It's not uncommon for me to work 12 to 14 hour days. The thought of cooking at the end of an exhausting workday is about as intriguing as joining the Polar Bear Club and jumping into frigid degree water. Yet, without that meal to bond us as a family each night, we all too often go our separate ways. My daughter will grab a snack here or there, I will eat while reading something from my briefcase and my husband will grab a bite on his way home from the office or just eat an extra-large lunch. Our few precious hours at home together, become invaded by diversions. But I noticed when I did cook (those two or three times a year) or when my mother would come over and cook, we would all sit around the table and talk and enjoy and share.

I truly think that one of the biggest problems facing the American family today is the loss of the family dinner hour. Think about it—decades ago we shared two, if not three, meals together daily. These were basically mini-family-meetings, nourishing both body and soul. Now, statistics show we are fortunate to sit down together twice a week—to share a meal, much less linger over it!

In the end, I accepted my friend's challenge to write a cookbook series. I tried a lot of recipes, variations and methods. More food saw the garbage disposal than the pages of this book. But you will find within these pages the best-of-the-best recipes. Each recipe has been carefully tested for taste and time-saving ability. In addition, I created the Five Rules of Rush Hour Recipes and posted them on my cupboard. Any recipe that made it into this book had to meet the strict guidelines found on the following page:

The Five Rules of Rush Hour Recipes:

1. All ingredients should be able to be pronounced accurately through the phonetic use of the English Language.

2. Each ingredient can be located in the market without engaging in a full scale scavenger hunt.

3. No list of ingredients shall be longer than the instructions.

4. Each recipe has to be durable enough to survive me, the Queen-of-Incapable-Cooking, and elicit a compliment at meal's end.

5. My finicky child will eat it—or some portion of it. I've learned not to be too picky on this one. Often I separate out part of the meal during preparation and customize it to her taste.

I dedicated myself to making this series one that you will cherish, love and refer to again and again. It has accomplished my aforementioned goals for a return to the family dinner hour and easy, healthy eating. I know it can for you, too, so let's move on to the recipes. This volume features those that quickly became our family's favorites.

In the Beginning...

Sides, Soups and Starters

Quick Recipe Index:

Potato Shapes	16
Sugar Carrots	17
Spastic Salsa	17
Aunt Joan's Popovers	17
Potato Salad in a Pinch	18
Chicken Dumpling Soup	19
Tasty Tortellini Soup	20
Quick Chips	20
Cheesy Scalloped Spuds	21
Marvelous Mushroom Rice	22
Quickslaw	22
Crazy for Couscous	23
Potato and Broccoli Bake	24

FAMILY FAVORITES

Potato Shapes

3 potatoes, rinsed and peeled (or scrubbed clean with skins left on)
cooking spray
salt

Preheat oven to 350 degrees. Wash potatoes and cut them into wedges length-wise. Or cut them into circle slices. Or cut them into rectangular McDonald's™-emulating shapes. Or, if you are real creative, cut them into circles and then give the kids tiny cookie cutters to cut out their own shapes. It doesn't really matter—just cut the potatoes. Spray potatoes with a bit of cooking spray and sprinkle with salt. Place on cookie sheet in a single layer and bake for 30-50 minutes, depending on the thickness.

FREEZING TIP: I bought a fun potato-peeler contraption from one of those "cooking parties". It looks like a vice and you mount it on your counter, toss on a potato and twirl the handle. Not only does it peel the potatoes quickly and easily, but it leaves cute little "curly fries" in its wake. These "curly fries" can be tossed into a freezer bag to be cooked for a quick, kid-friendly snack or side dish later. We're supposed to keep brand names to a minimum in books—so consider this a subliminal message... *you may want to browse www.pamperedchef.com if you are looking for a similar contraption for your own kitchen.*

Sugar Carrots

My Mom made these carrots as our "vegetable" one night. Not liking cooked carrots to begin with, I wasn't too excited by her choice. All that changed when I had my first bite. My daughter and I agreed that if this was counted as a vegetable, you could count us in!

1 large package fresh carrots
3-4 tablespoons butter
3-4 tablespoons brown sugar

Cut fresh, peeled carrots into julienne strips. Simmer in pan of water till just fork tender. Drain. Return carrots to pan and melt the butter and brown sugar over the carrots until well-glazed and evenly coated, cooking perhaps another minute or two.

Spastic Salsa

1 cup salsa (you choose the heat)
1 can Mexican corn
1 tablespoon sugar
1 chopped Jalapeno pepper
salt and pepper to taste

Mix all ingredients together and let sit 30 minutes before serving.

Aunt Joan's Popovers

1 cup flour
2 large eggs
1 tablespoon sugar
¼ teaspoon salt
1 tablespoon salad oil
1 cup milk

Slowly add ingredients into the bowl in order listed, mixing continuously until perfectly smooth. Fill non-stick muffin pans ¾ full. Bake at 400 degrees for 40 minutes if making large popovers, 30 minutes for smaller. Do not open the oven to peek, or the puffed popovers will deflate while cooking.

Potato-Salad in a Pinch

1 pound cooked and diced potatoes
4 tablespoons low-fat mayonnaise
4 teaspoons cider vinegar
¼ teaspoon pepper, dash of salt
  to taste

Mix in a bowl. Can't get much easier than this!

The Electronic Supermarket

Too busy to shop? Look no further, the Internet has come to the rescue of busy cooks once again. Virtual Supermarkets are popping up left and right. With a few clicks of a mouse, you can order your groceries online, save frequently used shopping lists, and have them delivered to your door. Consider entering the grocery list from this book for those crazy, busy weeks when traveling to the store isn't an option. The charges for electronic grocery shopping vary, but many sites offer very reasonable rates that are well worth the time you will save—not to mention the nutrition you will gain over other quick fix solutions—like pizza!

Here are a few popular stores you may want to investigate:

www.netgrocer.com
www.shopthepig.com
www.deandeluca.com
www.peapod.com
www.safeway.com
www.traderjoes.com

FAMILY FAVORITES

Chicken Dumpling Soup

Soup:
1½ pounds chicken breasts, cut into pieces
4 cans chicken broth (14.5 oz. each)
4 (broth) cans water
1 large onion, chopped
4 carrots, chopped
2 celery stalks, chopped
1 teaspoon salt
1 teaspoon garlic powder
½ teaspoon pepper
½ teaspoon chicken bouillon

Dumplings:
½ cup cottage cheese
2 tablespoons water
½ teaspoon salt
1 cup flour
3 egg whites

Brown chicken in a non-stick skillet. Add vegetables, broth, water and seasonings. Bring to a boil and then reduce heat and simmer for 30 minutes.

While soup cooks, beat egg whites and cottage cheese thoroughly. Next, add salt and water. Stir in the flour, a bit at a time, mixing well. Drop mixture by tablespoonfuls into the boiling soup. Cover and reduce heat, simmering for 15 minutes more, until dumplings are cooked.

For a quicker dumpling mix, use the recipe that can be found on the back of a box of Bisquick™.

If your kids aren't fond of dumplings, pour half the soup into a separate pot before adding dumplings. Substitute egg noodles and simmer for 15 minutes. Serve with oyster crackers for a guaranteed hit.

Tasty Tortellini Soup

1 (14.5 oz.) can diced tomatoes
1½ cups water
1½ cups chicken broth
½ teaspoon crushed dried basil
¼ teaspoon pepper
2 cups, choose from the following: frozen peas, diced carrots, frozen broccoli, cauliflower
7 oz. (roughly 1½ cups) refrigerated-type tortellini

Mix the first 5 ingredients in a saucepan and bring to a boil. Add tortellini and vegetables. Return to boiling and then reduce heat. Simmer uncovered for 5-7 minutes or until tortellini are tender.

Quick Chips

7 flour tortillas
½ envelope of taco seasoning
spray oil

Cut tortillas into 6 triangles each. Layer on a cookie sheet and spray with oil. Sprinkle with taco seasoning and bake at 400 degrees for 10 minutes.

USELESS TRIVIA

IN THE UNITED STATES, A POUND OF POTATO CHIPS COSTS TWO HUNDRED TIMES MORE THAN A POUND OF POTATOES.

Cheesy Scalloped Spuds

6 potatoes, peeled and sliced
3 tablespoons margarine, melted
½ teaspoon salt
¼ teaspoon pepper
1 cup Swiss or cheddar cheese, shredded
1 cup milk

Preheat oven to 425º. Coat a 9 x 13 baking dish with cooking spray. Arrange half of potato slices in dish. Pour half of margarine over potatoes. Add half of the salt, pepper and cheese. Repeat layers. Drizzle with additional melted margarine and top with additional shredded cheese. Bring milk to a low boil in a small saucepan and pour over the potato mixture. Bake for 40-50 minutes or until potatoes are tender.

How to Become A Certified Potato-Head

Is your child in love with the potato? Now he or she can join the "Spuddy Buddy Club". They'll enjoy a free membership certificate and can download some fun activities, plus enter Spuddy's Fan Club. To become a member log on to: www.idahopotato.com and click on Spuddy Buddy.

FAMILY FAVORITES

Marvelous Mushroom Rice

2 cups uncooked white rice
1 (10.75 oz.) can condensed cream of mushroom soup
1 cup vegetable broth
⅛ cup water
½ cup fresh mushrooms, sliced or a 4 oz. can of mushrooms
1 teaspoon dried oregano
¼ cup butter, melted
¼ teaspoon salt
⅛ teaspoon pepper

Preheat oven to 350 degrees. Stir rice, soup and broth together in a 2 quart casserole dish. Blend in all other ingredients. Bake for 35 to 40 minutes or until rice is tender.

Quickslaw

2 cups shredded cabbage
1 cup shredded carrots
¼ cup white sugar
⅓ cup chopped onion
1 cup mayonnaise
salt and pepper

Mix all ingredients in a large bowl. Season with salt and pepper. Refrigerate several hours or until chilled.

EAT YOUR VEGETABLES

RESEARCH SHOWS THAT ONLY 43% OF MEALS SERVED IN THE US INCLUDE VEGETABLES. IF ALL ELSE FAILS, TRY TO ENCOURAGE YOUR CHILD TO CELEBRATE NATIONAL EAT YOUR VEGETABLES DAY ON JUNE 17TH

Crazy for Couscous

1½ cups uncooked couscous
2½ cups water and ⅛ cup water
1½ cups chopped ham
½ cup sliced green onions
½ cup grated Parmesan cheese
1 (15.25 oz.) can of whole-kernel corn, drained
2 tablespoons olive oil
1 tablespoon Dijon mustard
1 teaspoon dried basil

Bring 2½ cups water to a boil and stir in couscous. Remove from heat and cover, letting stand for five minutes. Fluff couscous and then transfer into a bowl and add ham, onion, cheese and corn, stirring gently. In a small bowl, combine oil, basil, mustard, ⅛ cup water, and salt and pepper to taste. Stir with a whisk until blended. Pour over couscous mixture and toss gently to coat.

The word couscous scares some children (and some adults, for that matter.) If that happens to be the case in your household, you have this chef's permission to substitute elbow macaroni or instant rice instead.

> FACTS YOU WILL NEVER NEED TO KNOW
>
> THE AVERAGE AMERICAN FAMILY OF FOUR CONSUMES 6000 POUNDS OF FOOD PER YEAR!

Potato and Broccoli Bake

2 pounds baking potatoes, scrubbed, peeled, and halved
1 cup chopped broccoli
½ cup part-skim ricotta cheese
½ teaspoon salt
¼ teaspoon ground red pepper
1 (8-oz.) container sour cream
¾ cup cheddar cheese, shredded

Preheat oven to 375 degrees. Bring potatoes to a boil in a medium saucepan. Reduce heat and simmer 20 minutes or until tender. Drain potatoes, reserving 1 cup of the liquid. Return potatoes and liquid to pan; mash with a potato masher until slightly chunky.

Add chopped broccoli and next 4 ingredients to pan and stir well. Spoon potato mixture into a 9 x 13-inch baking dish coated with cooking spray. Bake for 30-40 minutes or until heated through. Sprinkle with cheddar cheese and bake an additional few minutes until cheese melts.

Put Your Best Spud Forward...

Small Potatoes are best for use in salads.
Medium Potatoes work well for just about anything—mashed, baked, fried, you name it.
Large potatoes are ideal for French fries or the "meal-in-itself" baked potato.

A Merry Middle...
Main Meals in Minutes

Quick Recipe Index:

Tantalizing Taco Salad	26
Parmesan Pasta Bowl	27
Let-me-Soak Chicken	28
Presto Pasta	29
The Other White Meat	30
Soup and Sandwich Stops:	
#1. The Big Dipper	34
#2. Make Mine A Melt	35
#3. The Super-Stack	36
Must-Have Meatloaf	37
Christmas Eve Chili	38
Delightfully Dijon Chicken	40
Sammy's Favorite Noodle Bake	41
Ultra-Quick Chicken and Rice	42
Super Stroganoff Supper	43
Chicken Cordon Blue	44
Turkey-Stuffing Casserole	45
"Pizza Pockets"	46
One Dish Meat and Potatoes	47
Mexi-Casserole	48
Quick Fix Salsa Chicken	48
In-a-Pinch Pork Chops	49
Pizza Bake	49
Fine Fettuccini	50
Shell Stuffer	50
Beef Mix	53
(Includes meatloaf, meatballs & Salisbury steak)	

FAMILY FAVORITES

Tantalizing Taco Salad

1 lb. lean ground beef
2 ½ cups chopped bell pepper (any color will do just fine)
1 ½ cup baked tortilla chips, crumbled
2 ½ cups bottled salsa, you choose the heat
2 ½ cups of fresh diced tomatoes
6 cups of chopped romaine lettuce
6 oz. of cheddar cheese (I like to use the reduced-fat, pre-shredded cheese for convenience and calorie-saving.)
¼ cup diced green onion
dollop of sour cream (I use non-fat or reduced-fat)

Cook the pepper and beef in a nonstick skillet over medium heat until beef is brown. Add the salsa and bring the mixture to simmer. Remove from heat and cover to keep warm.

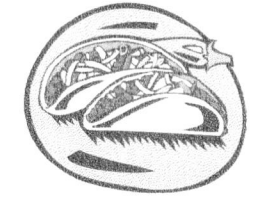

Place about 1 cup of lettuce on each of six individual plates. Top with 1/6th of the meat mixture and then sprinkle with 1/6th of the cheese, chips, and tomatoes. Top with a tablespoon of green onion, and a dollop of sour cream (if desired.)

If you are like me and have children that are "allergic" to all vegetables, remove a portion of the beef before adding peppers. Spread a few whole tortilla chip pieces on a plate and top with beef, then cheese. Microwave for 30 seconds to melt cheese— viola'—nachos. Or warm a flour tortilla in the oven and let them enjoy a soft cheese and beef taco or cheese quesadilla, without the peppers.

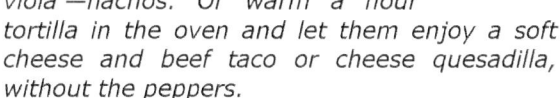

Parmesan Pasta Bowl

20 oz. of chicken broth
1 cup water
18 oz. of cooked chicken breast, cut into bite-sized pieces
2 cups of orzo (rice-shaped pasta)
1½ cup frozen peas, thawed
3 oz. Parmesan cheese (freshly grated is preferred)
salt and pepper

Pour chicken broth and 1 cup of water into a Dutch oven. Add chicken and orzo, then bring to a boil. Reduce heat, simmering for 12 minutes. Remove from heat and stir in the peas, ½ cup grated cheese, ½ teaspoon salt and ¼ teaspoon black pepper. Place in bowls and top with a bit more of the freshly grated Parmesan cheese. Serve with a loaf of French bread and whipped unsalted butter.

Click for Savings

Looking for a way to save money without clipping coupons? Try www.valuepage.com This online site allows you to enter your zip code, choose a supermarket, browse their weekly sales and specials, and then click the items you would like to save on. Print your list, hand it to the cashier and you will receive Web Bucks good for any purchase on your next visit

Note: Even if you consider yourself an Internet Novice, don't be afraid of this site. I promise it is simple and assessable to even the most inexperienced. After all, this is a Rush Hour Cook™ book—I promise not to include anything that takes more time than it's worth!

Let-Me-Soak Chicken

This is delicious when prepared on a grill!

olive oil or fat-free bottled Italian dressing
1 chicken breast for each person
fresh rosemary
1 lemon, cut into wedges
salt and pepper

Place chicken breasts in a shallow glass pan. Pour enough oil or bottled dressing to cover. Add sprigs of rosemary. Squeeze lemon over chicken then drop lemon rind into marinade mixture. Let sit for at least an hour—though the longer the better. (In my ideal world, I remember to do this in the morning and then we grill it that night.)

To cook: grill for a delicious flavor—five minutes on each side or until done, basting with marinade. Or toss it in a frying pan and do the same. Bake for 30 minutes. Discard any uncooked marinade! Serve with a side salad and French bread.

Edible Finger-paints

Next time you are looking for a way to occupy Junior while cooking, try this quick tip from the author of *365 Quick, Easy and Inexpensive Dinner Menus*. Mix up a box of vanilla instant pudding and divide it into several bowls. Lay down a sheet of wax paper. Let your child add a few drops of food coloring to each of the vanilla pudding dishes. Now encourage creativity by letting your child finger-paint on the waxed paper with the pudding mixtures. When finished, discard waxed paper, lick fingers and enjoy. Make sure your children wash their hands before this project.

Presto Pasta

9 oz. uncooked angel hair pasta
3 cups broccoli florets
1 (10-oz.) jar of Alfredo Sauce (I like the low-fat one that is made by Five Brothers®)
1½ cups of diced ham
Parmesan cheese, freshly grated

Cook pasta in boiling water for 4 minutes. Add broccoli to pasta and cook another minute. Drain. Add ham, sauce and cook until broccoli is fork tender. Salt and pepper to taste. Serve onto plates and top with Parmesan cheese.

Breadsticks always work well with pasta. You can purchase delicious Italian breadsticks in most grocery stores, or use a roll of breadstick dough from the refrigerator section of your local market.

Young kids are always eager to help cook when the recipe involves dough.

Add Some Spice to Your Life!

More for fun than a Freudian study, here are what some popular herbs represent:

Basil	Love (or hate)
Bay	Victory
Lavender	Acknowledgement
Fennel	Praise
Caraway	Retention
Marjoram	Happiness
Mint	Wisdom
Rosemary	Remembrance
Sage	Long Life
Thyme	Bravery

So the next time you are feeling under the weather, stock up on the marjoram!

The Other White Meat

While pork is often overlooked, it's an affordable and tasty alternative when you are tired of the typical poultry.

6 bone-in pork chops (the inexpensive ones are fine)
3 teaspoons olive oil
2 cups dry white cooking wine (or chicken broth)
½ cup honey
½ cup Dijon mustard

Heat oil in nonstick skillet over medium heat. Add pork and cook on each side for five minutes or until browned. Remove the chops from the pan. Place wine or broth, honey and mustard in the pan and bring to a boil. Simmer sauce for 2-3 minutes. Return pork to the pan and simmer for 10-12 minutes, turning halfway through, until meat is fully cooked.

A Couple Quick Tips from www.gourmettips.com

When cooking with wine, leave the pan uncovered so the alcohol will burn off. The resulting liquid will have a rounder, firmer, fruitier flavor.

For flat, perfectly cooked bacon, lay strips on a sheet pan and bake in a 350 degree oven until crisp, 15 to 20 minutes. Drain on paper towels.

You can visit www.gourmettips.com for over 500 quick and wonderful tips to make your cooking easier and tastier!

From the Toolbox of Tips

It has been said that changing one's mind is a woman's prerogative. However, I don't think the author of that statement anticipated how often women change their minds on what to fix for dinner during the course of a day.

My routine goes like this... get up at some early hour in order to get everyone else up at a normal hour, then think about breakfast. Schlep cereal on the table and run to work. Half way through the day, it occurs to me I will need to create dinner for my family. At this point, usually whatever my coworker ate for lunch seems a good candidate. By 3 o'clock, I'm usually starving from not having time to eat yet, so my dinner choices turn to richer foods—like a stack of flapjacks or a juicy bacon cheeseburger. When I leave work, I go by the store and think about stopping—but alas I am too exhausted. I justify that I can just "throw" something together from the pantry. (I ignore the fact that my last five attempts to throw something together have ended up in the garbage, untouched.) I get home only to scour through the pantry and learn that I can make spaghetti and meatballs—if only I had spaghetti; macaroni and cheese—if only I had cheese, chicken with lemon and rosemary—if only I had the chicken. What's a girl to do? And of course, you know how this story ends—the famed call to the takeout place up the street.

One of the best techniques I've found to streamline supper is to simply assign each night a predetermined "theme." Now, some of you may be organized enough that this isn't necessary, but for those of us who have found all-too-much comfort in the cardboard of a takeout box, this is a winning strategy.

Take a weekly calendar and next to each day of the week, write down a theme for the evening. Below you'll find examples from my own cooking calendar.

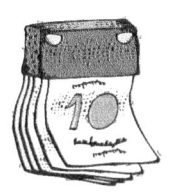

For example:

Finger Foods
This could be appetizer trays of fruit, vegetables, cheese and crackers, mini-sandwiches, hot dogs on sticks—anything that can be tackled by hand... literally!

Breakfast for Dinner
If your family is at all like mine, a leisurely breakfast of omelets, pancakes, sausage and accompaniments only occurs when you are traveling or hitting the Sunday brunch buffet. Try doing a breakfast for dinner. Eggs and pancakes are quick and easy to prepare and by doing them in the evening everyone can enjoy them before racing off to their appointed destinations.

Pasta Presto
You pick the type and the night for Pasta Presto. Perhaps it's spaghetti, fettuccini, macaroni, lasagna—just pick a sauce and pasta and check a weeknight off your list.

Meat and Potatoes
Unless you are a vegetarian, it's best to designate at least one night for the good ol' American standby.

Some Assembly Required
Whether it's pizza, tacos or baked potatoes, this night features a main course that each family member can customize to their liking.

Kid's Cook
(or spouse cooks, or mailman cooks)—You get the picture—someone other than Mom gets to man the kitchen (and the dishes) for this night.

Soup & Sandwich
There is a reason almost every restaurant offers a soup and sandwich special—it's a hearty, healthy and wholesome combo!

Make It and Bake It
When in a rush there is nothing like the beloved casserole. Choose your favorite, throw it together, and toss it in the oven for a 30-minute-bake. Don't forget to double your recipe and reserve one for freezing.

Lasso Your Leftovers
I dedicate this theme to my mother. For years, my mother has insisted on saving food—never wasting a biteful. While I find this quality admirable, I find it interesting how much food is wrapped carefully in plastic so tightly it could be donated to NASA, only to sit in my refrigerator for longer than George Burns was alive. This night is dedicated for anyone else who hoards their leftovers—now is the time to bring 'em out and bring 'em on.

Deal With It Dinner
I must confess, this is one of my favorite themes. It basically involves letting someone else deal with the cooking or letting the family forage for their own findings in the fridge.

Soup & Sandwich Stop #1: The Big Dipper

6 hoagie rolls
1 tablespoon butter
¾ lb. lean roast beef, sliced
1 package au jus dry mix
*1 small onion, sliced into rings
*1 small can mushrooms

If sharing this meal with children, make sure to cook onion and mushrooms in separate pan and avoid touching the other foods at all costs.

Melt 1 tablespoon of butter or margarine in a nonstick skillet over medium heat. Add mushrooms and onions and sauté for two minutes. Add roast beef and a ⅛ cup of the au jus. Reduce heat to low and cook until heated through.

While beef is heating, lightly butter the hoagie rolls and toast them in separate skillet or under broiler until golden brown.

Place one hoagie roll on each plate, and then pile on some of the roast beef mixture. Put a bit of au jus in a small serving dish on the side. (You will avoid confrontation with children by letting each child have their own little "dipping" bowl.) Serve with a soup of your choice.

Mail a Meal

Next time you are looking for a fun and inexpensive way to say "hello," try a mail-a-meal postcard. This service allows you to choose from hundreds of recipe postcards. Simply type in your e-mail recipient, your message, and click send. (I must confess, I sent a few postcards to myself.)

Soup & Sandwich Stop #2
Make-Mine-A Melt

6 bagel halves or slices of French bread
1 lb. shaved turkey or ham
6 slices of Swiss or cheddar cheese
  butter or margarine

Lightly butter bread and brown over medium-low heat in a nonstick skillet. Transfer bread onto cookie sheet. Top each slice of bread with meat and then cheese. Bake in a 350 degree oven until cheese melts. Serve with your favorite soup.

You may also want to try:
Pizza—Spread tomato sauce over the bread and top with mozzarella cheese and pepperoni

Veggie—Top with mushrooms, onion, broccoli and cheese

Tuna—Spread with tuna and top with cheese

> ### A Blast from the Past...
>
> Oh...the good ol' days! Look at this weekly food budget from 1918...
>
> | | |
> |---|---|
> | Grain Foods | $2.50 |
> | Milk | $2.00 |
> | Meat, Eggs and Fish | $2.00 |
> | Fruits and Veggies | $2.00 |
> | Fats, Sugar and Misc. | $1.50 |
>
> from *The Business of the Household* by C.W. Taber, Published in 1918

Soup & Sandwich Stop #3
The Super-Stack

6 slices of bread
½ pound of deli sliced turkey
½ pound of deli sliced ham
6 thin slices of Alpine Lace Cheese (a nice low-fat alternative to Swiss, you'll find it in the deli)
1 can cream of mushroom soup

Set oven to broil. Toast bread in toaster and then place on cookie sheet. In a nonstick skillet, warm turkey and ham over medium heat. In a separate sauce pan, pour soup and ½ can water. Pile turkey and ham onto toast. Top with a slice of Alpine Lace Swiss Cheese and broil until cheese is melted. Transfer each sandwich to a plate. Top with mushroom soup. Serve with your favorite soup.

If kids realize you are using cream of mushroom soup with this sandwich, screaming may occur. To avoid this, simply leave the soup off of their sandwich altogether and substitute a slice of American cheese, that "other yellow cheese" (instead of cheddar or Swiss) to further increase this recipe's kid-friendliness.

Make a Must-Have List

Using a magnet, place a large blank sheet of paper on your fridge. Throughout the week, write down all the must-have items in your household. Include everything from toiletries to kitchen items. Make photocopies of this list. When you go shopping, use this list as an "inventory" to figure out what items you need. This is also a great way to "prompt" your memory for other items to pick up when you make an impromptu grocery store stop. Keep a copy in each of your car's glove boxes for quick and handy reference.

Must-Have Meatloaf

1 cup chopped onion
1 teaspoon pepper
1 teaspoon salt
4 garlic cloves, minced
1 egg, beaten
¾ cup Italian-seasoned breadcrumbs
1 pound lean ground turkey
1 (8-oz.) can of tomato sauce

Preheat oven to 350 degrees. Combine first 6 ingredients in a bowl. Add meat and blend slightly. Form the mixture into a loaf and place in a 9 x 5 inch pan coated with cooking spray. Spread tomato sauce over the top of the loaf and bake for 1 hour or until cooked through. Let stand for 10 minutes before slicing.

Note: If you haven't tried lean ground turkey as a substitute for beef, I encourage you to give it a try. I am quite stubborn and have always insisted "it could never taste as good as beef." Then my husband snuck it into several meals. I quickly changed my tune.

Don't forget to toss a child's main vegetable-group on the table... ketchup. You can also substitute ⅓ cup of ketchup for the tomato sauce.

This is a great cook ahead meal. Instead of preparing just one, make a couple of extras. Wrap in aluminum foil and freeze. When you are ready to use them, remove them from the freezer in the morning or the night before. By evening they will be thawed. Bake as instructed above—or a bit longer if meat is still cold when placed in oven. Don't forget to write the date on your frozen meal—these will keep for up to 3 months.

Christmas-Eve Chili

8 Servings

Always a bit rebellious, my family started a tradition of making Chili on Christmas Eve when we realized that the thought of making a large meal with tons of dishes didn't seem appealing the day before the big event! We've tried many recipes over the years, all fighting for the title of "Christmas Chili Captain." Here is our favorite so far…

2 pounds lean ground beef
2 (14.5-oz.) cans Mexican-style stewed tomatoes
1 tablespoon sugar
1 small can tomato paste
½ teaspoon cumin
¼ teaspoon salt

Choose as many as you like:
1 cup onion, chopped
2 cloves minced garlic
1 can corn
1 (14.5-oz.) can kidney beans
1 tablespoon red pepper flakes
⅛ cup jalapenos
   (include the juice if you like it really hot!)
1 red bell pepper, chopped
1 green pepper, chopped
3 tablespoons chili powder
1 tablespoon oregano
1 tablespoon basil leaves
1 tablespoon Cajun spice mix

Choose one:
1 cup red wine
1 bottle of beer
1 cup of coffee
1 cup beef broth

Choose one "secret" ingredient…
1 tablespoon brown sugar (instead of white)
3 Hershey Kisses™ (or substitute chocolate chips or 1 tablespoon cocoa)
1 teaspoon instant coffee
¼ teaspoon cinnamon

Choose one (or none!)
instant white rice
elbow macaroni

Brown meat in a large skillet over medium heat. Drain. If you have chosen garlic or onion, add them to the meat and cook another minute or two. Add all other ingredients you have chosen, stirring well. Cook on medium heat for 5-10 minutes and then reduce heat to low for at least 40 minutes. Of course, as with most soups, stews and chili recipes—the longer they cook, the more the flavors meld! For great tasting flavor, try putting this recipe together in the morning and then simmer it in a slow cooker all day on a low setting for a great dinner meal. If desired, prepare rice or macaroni in a separate pan. Mix into chili prior to serving, or place in bottom of individual bowls and pour chili over the top. Garnish with shredded cheese and sour cream. Tastes even better the following day so make sure to make some extra!

Facts You Will Never Need to Know

Don Juan de Ornate entered what is now New Mexico in 1598 and brought with him the green chili pepper. It has grown there for nearly 400 years since.– *The International Chili Society*

FAMILY FAVORITES

Delightfully Dijon Chicken

½ cup breadcrumbs
2 teaspoons Italian seasoning
½ teaspoon salt
½ teaspoon pepper
3 tablespoons Dijon mustard
6 chicken breasts
1 tablespoon olive oil or margarine

Combine first four ingredients in a shallow pan and mix well. Brush the mustard on both sides of each chicken breast and then dredge in seasoning mixture. Heat oil in a skillet over medium heat. Add chicken, cooking 6 minutes on each side or until cooked through. Serve with your favorite side dishes.

Tried and True Timesavers

If you can plan your recipes ahead of time, you can do several steps at once. For example, if you are going to use 3 onions, why not chop them all together? While this does require a bit of foresight it spares precious minutes later in the week.

Use the grocery list at the back of this book as a guideline of items to have on hand. It's not very long, and if you use it as a checklist, you can feel confident that you can open a Rush Hour Cook™ book and prepare many of the recipes within each volume.

Keep a jar of minced garlic on hand to avoid having to mince your own.

Sammy's Favorite Noodle Bake

Before I became the Rush Hour Cook™, there were two recipes that my family would actually request that I prepare—(the rest of the time they banned me from the kitchen.) Below, you'll find one of them.

1 package of penne pasta
1 container fat-free ricotta cheese
1 bag of part-skim mozzarella cheese
1 pound lean ground beef
3 garlic cloves, minced
1 jar prepared spaghetti sauce (Ragu™, etc.)
1 cup chopped onion
1 cup sliced mushrooms

Preheat oven to 350 degrees. Cook pasta according to directions. While pasta is cooking, brown beef over medium heat in a nonstick skillet. Drain.

Add mushrooms, onion and garlic. Return to heat and cook for 2-3 more minutes or until onion is transparent. Add the jar of spaghetti sauce and simmer over low heat for 10 minutes. While this is simmering, combine container of ricotta cheese and ⅔ of your mozzarella cheese in a bowl.

Drain noodles. Spray a baking dish with cooking spray and then layer your ingredients, beginning with a pasta layer on the bottom. Cover with meat, then cheese. Repeat layers. Bake for 30 minutes. Top with additional mozzarella cheese and bake for another 5 minutes or until cheese is melted and bubbly. Serve with a warm loaf of French bread.

If kids will be dining with you this evening, this is your last chance to reserve some browned beef to keep separate from the forthcoming onion, mushrooms and garlic. I usually reserve ½ cup for my daughter, and then mix and bake hers separately. If your child is a spaghetti lover, consider making this recipe for the adults and reserving some noodles and plain sauce for a separate spaghetti plate.

Sammy's Favorite Noodle Bake is also a great recipe for bulk preparation and freezing. I usually divide the bake into two dishes. I cook one and then package the other for the freezer. You can also purchase individual-serving-size aluminum tins at your local grocer. Use these tins to make individual bake servings that can be cooked up for lunch or on nights when people are "eating on the run."

Ultra-Quick Chicken and Rice

4 boneless chicken breasts
1 can (10.75 oz.) cream of chicken soup
1 ⅔ cup water
½ teaspoon pepper
½ cup instant white rice, uncooked
2 cups broccoli florets (fresh or frozen)

Brown chicken in a skillet over medium heat. Remove from pan. Pour soup, water and seasoning into the pan and then heat to boiling. Stir in instant rice and broccoli. Place chicken on top of mixture. Cover and cook over low heat for 5-10 minutes or until cooked through.

You can also prepare this recipe with any other cream soup—cream of mushroom, cream of broccoli, etc.

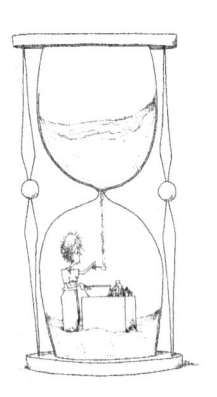

Super Stroganoff Supper

According to *Cook's Illustrated*, the essential problem with stroganoff is that since it's made with a pan sauce, not as a slow braise or stew, it doesn't have time to develop much flavor. Instead of slathering the meal with spices and extra ingredients to increase flavor, they offer a few simple tips...
- Cut beef sirloin into thin strips—not thick.
- Brown the mushrooms in pan before the beef.
- Use white wine rather than red—consider adding a bit of chicken or beef broth, as well.
- Use onions in place of shallots.

I have incorporated these tips into my favorite recipe below. You'll love this... and it's good for you, too! Who says great tasting dishes can't be low in fat?

1 ½ pound sirloin, cut into THIN strips
3 tablespoons flour, if using broth
1 (12 oz.) jar of beef gravy or broth
3 cloves minced garlic
½ teaspoon salt
¼ teaspoon sugar
¼ teaspoon pepper
1 cup of fresh mushrooms, sliced
¾ cup sour cream (nonfat or low fat)
½ bag of egg noodles

Cook egg noodles according to package directions. Drain. Brown mushrooms and remove from pan. Brown meat in same nonstick skillet. Sift flour into small bowl, add broth, and whisk well to avoid lumps. Add broth/flour mixture to skillet. Add garlic and seasonings. Continue stirring over low heat until meat is cooked and sauce is smooth. Return mushrooms to the mixture. Lastly add sour cream, stirring gently until heated through. Serve over egg noodles.

You may want to forego the mushrooms to make this even more kid-friendly.

FAMILY FAVORITES

Chicken Cordon Bleu

6 chicken breasts
6 slices of ham
3 tablespoons skim milk
¼ cup bread crumbs
6 slices of Alpine Lace cheese sliced into ½" strips

Preheat oven to 400 degrees. Cut an insert into each chicken breast.* Roll a slice of ham around a ½ inch strip of the cheese and stuff into middle. Roll chicken in milk and then dredge in breadcrumbs. Place on a pan sprayed with cooking oil and bake for 25-30 minutes or until done. Add enough cheese to cover chicken, and return to oven until cheese is melted and bubbly.

*You can also use a meat mallet to flatten the chicken breast between two sheets of wax paper. Then place ham and cheese on breast and roll up tortilla fashion. Roll chicken in milk, dredge in breadcrumbs and place seam side down on pan. Continue as above.

Potato Resuscitation 101

If you find yourself with lumpy, gummy or pasty potatoes—never fear. As a Rush Hour Cook™ Specialist one of my many talents is resuscitating what looks to be ruined food. Simply stir in three tablespoons of minced onion and an egg yolk (beaten.) Form into ½ inch pancake shapes, 3 inches crosswise. Cook in a tad of butter over medium-high heat until nicely browned for perfect potato patties!

FAMILY FAVORITES

Turkey and Stuffing Casserole

1 small onion, chopped
3 stalks of celery, chopped
3 cups of chicken broth (2 cups for first half of recipe, 1 cup for second part of recipe)
9 oz. of unseasoned stuffing-mix cubes
1½ pound turkey breast, cut into strips
½ teaspoon thyme
salt and pepper to taste
2 tablespoons flour

Preheat oven to 350 degrees. Combine onion, celery and 2 cups of broth in a saucepan over medium heat. Cover and simmer until vegetables are soft. Add stuffing and thyme and mix well. Spray a 9 x 13 casserole dish with cooking oil and then spread stuffing mixture evenly along bottom of dish. Top with turkey strips.

In a separate, microwave-safe container, mix 1 cup broth with flour and whisk well. Cook on high for 2-3 minutes, stirring occasionally. Pour mixture over turkey. Sprinkle with parsley, if desired. Cover and bake for 25-30 minutes or until turkey is done.

Useless Turkey Trivia:

In 1995, 295 million turkeys were raised in the United States... That translates into 6.61 billion pounds of live turkey, or 5.2 billion pounds of ready-to-cook turkey. Americans consume about 15 percent of those birds, or 44 million turkeys, at Thanksgiving. About 7.3 percent are consumed at Christmas and 6.3 percent at Easter. The world's heaviest turkey on record weighs 86 pounds—about the size of a large German Shepherd.

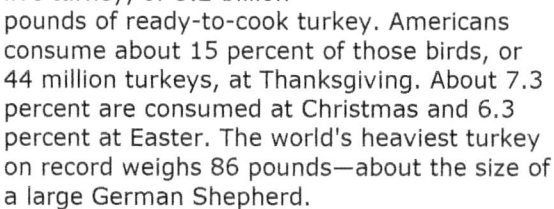

Pizza Pockets

Makes about 10 "pockets"

1 (10-oz.) package of refrigerated pizza crust
1 teaspoon of olive oil
½ cup mozzarella cheese
¼ teaspoon garlic salt
4 oz. of pizza sauce
toppings of your choice—mushrooms, pepperoni, onions, sausage, etc.

Preheat oven to 400 degrees. Cut pizza dough in half and roll out one half. Brush with olive oil and then sprinkle with the garlic salt. Spread pizza sauce over dough and top with mozzarella cheese. Add any additional ingredients of your choice. Roll out the other half of pizza dough and cover with top crust. Pinch the edges to seal. Bake 12-18 minutes, or until crust is browned.

If each person wants different ingredients, cut the pizza crust into separate pieces. Roll out the other half of the dough and then place on top of ingredients, squeezing the edges to form "pockets".

Variations: You can make this same recipe substituting a slice of thick French bread for the pizza dough. Then add sauce, ingredients, etc. Top with mozzarella cheese and broil until cheese has melted.

Americans eat approximately 100 acres of pizza EACH DAY, or about 350 slices per second.

Each man, woman and child in America eats an average of 23 pounds of pizza per year.

FAMILY FAVORITES

One-Dish Meat and Potatoes

Turkey loaf:
1 pound lean ground turkey
½ cup dry breadcrumbs
⅓ cup ketchup
⅓ cup onion, chopped
1 egg
2 cloves of minced garlic
½ teaspoon salt
½ teaspoon pepper

Potatoes:
1½ pounds potatoes
5 garlic cloves, minced
⅓ cup sour cream
2 tablespoons milk
1 teaspoon salt

Preheat oven to 350 degrees. Place a large pot of water on high heat for potatoes.

Mix all ingredients for the turkey loaf together. Press meat mixture into a 9" pie plate that has been coated with cooking spray. Bake for 25 minutes.

Rinse, peel and then cut potatoes into small slices. (Remember the smaller you cut them, the quicker they will cook!) Cook potatoes until soft, drain. Place potatoes and all other potato ingredients into a mixing bowl. Mash and mix together.

When 25 minutes have passed, spread potato mixture over the turkey loaf. Return to oven and bake an additional 10-20 minutes or until top is lightly browned. Cut into 6 wedges and serve by the wedge with your favorite vegetable.

Mexi-Casserole

This is one of our ultimate favorites—it's quick and has less than 3 grams of fat per serving!

6 ounces elbow macaroni, uncooked
1 pound lean ground beef or turkey
3 (14.5 oz.) cans diced tomatoes, undrained
12 oz. canned corn, undrained
2 packages of taco seasoning mix

Cook pasta according to package directions. Coat a Dutch oven with cooking spray. Brown meat over medium heat until it crumbles. Drain pasta. Stir pasta, tomatoes, corn and seasonings together. Cook five minutes.

Quick-Fix Salsa Chicken

12 oz. of wagon wheel pasta, uncooked
36 oz. of thick and chunky salsa (You choose the heat.)
12 oz. of diced chicken breast
4 oz. of Monterey Jack Cheese

Cook pasta according to package directions. Lightly brown chicken pieces and then combine with salsa in a skillet over medium heat. Cook until chicken is done. Place drained pasta on each plate and then top with chicken/salsa mixture.

In-A-Pinch Pork Chops

6 boneless pork chops (the inexpensive ones are fine)
¾ cup balsamic vinegar
½ cup chicken broth
2 cloves garlic
⅛ teaspoon pepper

Cook chops in a skillet over medium heat—about 5 to 10 minutes on each side, depending on thickness. Remove and place one chop on each plate. Place all other ingredients in skillet and stir until it becomes a thin sauce—about 5 minutes. Spoon over chops and serve with mashed potatoes.

Pizza Bake

1 pound lean ground beef or turkey
1 (15 oz.) can chunky tomato sauce
1 (10 oz.) package of refrigerated pizza crust dough
6 slices of mozzarella cheese
⅛ teaspoon oregano
⅛ teaspoon thyme
⅛ teaspoon pepper

Cook meat over medium heat until browned, then add tomato sauce and cook until heated. In a 9 x 13 casserole dish, unroll pizza crust dough and press into bottom and sides of casserole dish. Line pizza dough with ½ of the mozzarella cheese slices. Top with meat mixture. Bake in a 400 degree oven for 12-15 minutes. Top with remaining mozzarella cheese and bake for an additional 5-7 minutes or until cheese melts.

Fine Fettuccini

This recipe moves along quickly since you can complete most of the steps to make the sauce while your noodles are cooking.

1 (12-oz.) package fettuccini noodles
5 cloves minced garlic
1 cup white wine (or chicken broth)
½ cup fat-free half and half
2 tablespoons flour
½ teaspoon salt
½ teaspoon pepper
1 cup grated Parmesan cheese (freshly grated is all the better!)

Cook pasta according to directions. Drain. Melt a little butter over medium heat and sauté garlic for two minutes. Add wine and cook for another 4-5 minutes. Combine 4 tablespoons half-and-half and flour and stir until smooth. Add to wine mixture and stir well. Add remaining half-and-half, salt and pepper. Stir constantly for five minutes or until thickened. Toss pasta with sauce mixture and freshly grated Parmesan cheese.

Shell Stuffers

15 oz. package jumbo shell pasta (about 24 shells)
1 cup non-fat ricotta cheese
1 cup part skim ricotta cheese
1 (10-oz.) package frozen spinach, thawed and chopped
1 (28 oz.) jar spaghetti sauce

Preheat oven to 350 degrees. Cook pasta according to directions. Drain. Combine cheeses and spinach in a bowl. Fill pasta shells with a spoonful of mixture. Spread ½ cup spaghetti sauce in the bottom of a 9 x 13 inch pan. Place shells in baking dish and top with remaining sauce. Cover and bake for 30-35 minutes.

The Art of Bulk Cooking

If you are looking for a way to revolutionize the way you cook, consider bulk cooking for the freezer. One of our company's best-selling authors, Deborah Taylor-Hough, has taken this cooking method and made it into an exact science, allowing families throughout the world to spend less time in the kitchen and more time at the family table. Here are a few tips on how you, too, can enjoy this method!

Deborah advises that you sit down with a blank calendar and choose your recipes for 30 days. Consider how many times your family will eat the same meal twice. For example, can you get away with serving lasagna 3 times in 30 days? If so, pencil it in. Once you have all your recipes written down, create a master list of ingredients. Use that as your shopping list. Do all your prep-work (cutting, dicing, etc.) for all the recipes the night before your cook day. Then, move through the process of preparing and packaging all the foods on the following day. As you complete each recipe, use a black permanent marker to write the date frozen and any additional preparation needs. For example: "Top with 1 cup cheese and bake for 40 minutes at 350 degrees." This will make it easier for others to prepare the meals when you are unavailable—and avoid scavenging for recipes and instructions when it comes time for preparation.

There is an art to freezer cooking though, so if it is really of interest to you, I encourage you to pick up *Frozen Assets: how to cook for a day and eat for a month* or *Frozen Assets Lite and Easy*. She shows you how to cook the meals partially and then complete the cooking process when you reheat the meal—that avoids the leftover-taste that scares most people from this method. In any event, on the following page, is one great, versatile recipe from her book, excerpted from *Frozen Assets,* (ISBN 1-891400-61-4, www.championpress.com)

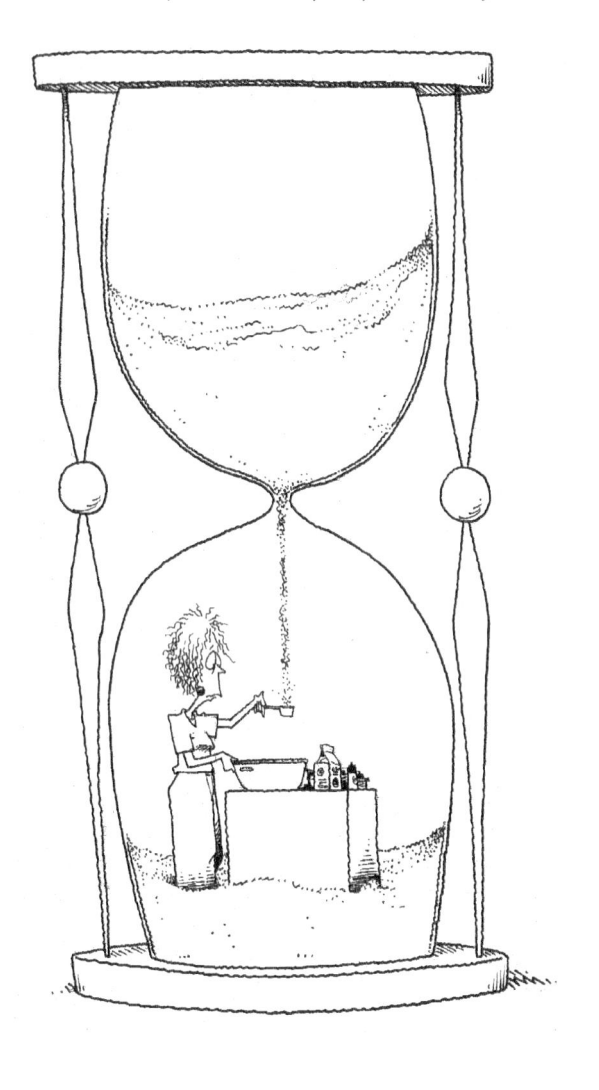

Beef Mix

The versatile recipe below gives you everything you need to prepare 2 meatloaves and 1 Salisbury Steak meal, or 3 meals of meatballs (to use with pasta sauces, meatball sandwiches, etc.)

24 ounces tomato sauce
3 cups dry bread crumbs
7 eggs, lightly beaten
1 cup onion, finely chopped
½ green pepper, finely chopped
2 teaspoons salt (optional)
¼ teaspoon dried thyme, crushed
¼ teaspoon dried marjoram, crushed
8 pounds ground beef

Combine first eight ingredients. Add ground beef and mix well. Divide meat mixture in half.

For Meatloaf: shape half the mixture into two loaves and place in a high-sided baking dish. Don't allow the loaves to touch. Bake at 350 degrees for one hour. Cool. Wrap individually in heavy-duty foil, label and freeze. To serve, thaw loaves and bake in 350 degree oven for 30 minutes or until heated through.

For Meatballs: Shape into meatballs and place on broiler pan so grease can drain while cooking. Bake uncovered in 350 degree oven for 30 minutes. Cool. Divide into three meal sized portions. To prevent from freezing into a solid meatball-mass, pre-freeze individually on cookie sheets and then place in freezer bags. Label and freeze. To serve, thaw and reheat with your choice of sauce.

For Salisbury Steak: Form half the meat mixture into oval ½ inch thick patties. Heat oil in nonstick skillet over medium heat until hot. Place beef patties in skillet; cook seven to eight minutes or until centers are no longer pink, turning once. Cool. Place in freezer bags; freeze. To serve, thaw and reheat with one (10 ¾ ounce) can cream of mushroom soup poured over as sauce. Serve with rice or noodles.

A Sweet & Happy Ending...
Delectable Desserts

Quick Recipe Index:

Banana Cream Pie	56
No Bake Scrumptious Chocolate Peanut Butter Squares	56
Skinny Pancakes	57
Gramma Harriett's "Red Hot" Apple Crisp	58
Manic for Maple Butter!	58
Champion Chocolate Cookies	59
Fanciful Fruit Dream	60
Baked Cinnamon Apples	60
You Choose-the-Chip Cookies	61
Chocolate Dipped Strawberry's	61
Cinnamon Streusel Coffee Cake	62
Snicker™ Bar Salad	62

Banana Cream Pie

1 prepared package of vanilla pudding—but only use 1⅔ cups milk
4 oz. of vanilla yogurt
2 cups of sliced bananas
20-30 vanilla wafers
2 cups whipped topping

Add yogurt to prepared pudding. Line an 8 inch pie pan with half of the vanilla wafers. Arrange bananas over wafers. Prop the rest of the wafers up around the side of the pan. Pour in pudding mixture. Top with whipped topping. Refrigerate until firm, at least two hours.

No-Bake Scrumptious Chocolate Peanut-Butter Squares
Makes about 2 dozen

1 cup corn syrup
1 cup white sugar
1½ cups peanut butter
8 cups crisp rice cereal
1 cup semisweet chocolate chips

Grease a 9 x 13 baking pan. Mix sugar, syrup, and peanut butter in a microwave-safe bowl. Microwave on high for two to three minutes or until boiling. Remove carefully (mixture will be hot) and stir in cereal and chips until coated. Transfer mixture to greased pan. Press down the mix until flat and even. Once cool, cut into squares and serve.

Skinny Pancakes

Makes 4 Servings

One thing that I could always cook was this crepe recipe passed down from my grandparents. My grandmother invented this recipe during the depression when eggs were sparse and she was trying to stretch every ingredient. Although a very different texture than today's traditional crepes, this has remained a family favorite and I continue to prepare it regularly.

Makes about 4-6 large, crepe-style pancakes
1 cup milk
1 cup flour
1 egg
1 "hollow palm" of salt

Whisk all four ingredients together in a bowl. Spray a skillet with cooking oil and warm the pan over medium heat. Pour one large spoonful of the batter into the skillet, then lift skillet by handle and rotate to "spread" the batter around the bottom of the pan. The crepe will be very thin, almost transparent in some places. Cook until golden on each side. Stack these on a plate in a warm oven while cooking the rest of the batter. Although syrup can always be used, consider using my favorite combination of a nice, big, dollop of real butter and some sugar and cinnamon. Then roll the crepe like you would a soft taco, pick up, and enjoy!

> **More Useless Trivia**
> Americans eat 20.7 pounds of candy per person annually. The Dutch eat three times as much.

FAMILY FAVORITES

Gramma Harriet's 'Red Hot' Apple Crisp

6-8 Granny Smith apples, peeled
¼ cup Red Hot™ cinnamon candies
½ cup butter
1 cup sugar
¾ cup flour

Preheat oven to 350 degrees. Cut apples into ¼ " thick slices. Arrange in a 9 x 13 buttered baking dish. Sprinkle on the Red Hot™ candies. Mix butter, sugar and flour till crumbly and then cover the top. Bake for 40-45 minutes, until bubbly.

Manic for Maple Butter!

WARNING: This recipe has been known to cause incredibly strong cravings for "more!" with those who consume it.

I have learned to control my consumption of this rich and wonderful butter to the holiday season. At the first sight of winter, you'll find my mother busily assembling the maple butter while the rest of us drool in wait!

1 stick unsalted butter, softened to room temperature–but not too soft! (This is very important or the recipe will not work.)
¼ teaspoon maple flavoring
4 teaspoons dark brown sugar
½ cup PURE maple syrup (not the cheap stuff)

With an electric mixer, beat the first three ingredients until fluffy. Continue beating while slowly drizzling in the PURE maple syrup until smooth and totally blended. Can store in fridge up to 3 weeks.

Excellent on popovers, English muffins, toast and crumpets. Makes a great homemade, holiday gift in place of the proverbial paperweight fruitcake.

FAMILY FAVORITES

Champion Chocolate Cookies

Makes about 2 dozen

1 (18.25-oz.) package light devil's food cake mix
2 tablespoons butter, softened
2 tablespoons water
2 large egg whites
1 large egg
¾ cup semi-sweet chocolate chips
cooking spray

Preheat oven to 350 degrees. Combine first 5 ingredients in large bowl. Beat with a hand mixer at medium speed for 2 minutes. Stir in chips. Spray cookie sheets with cooking oil. Drop by rounded teaspoons, 2 inches apart, onto baking sheets. Bake in preheated oven for 10 minutes. Cool on wire racks.

> **CHOCOLATE CRAVINGS**
>
> CONSUMERS SPEND MORE THAN $7 BILLION A YEAR ON CHOCOLATE. ANNUAL PER CAPITA CONSUMPTION OF CHOCOLATE IS 12 POUNDS PER PERSON. EACH AMERICAN EATS AN AVERAGE OF 51 POUNDS OF CHOCOLATE PER YEAR.

Fanciful Fruit Dream
8 servings

1 (6 oz.) pkg. orange flavored gelatin mix
2 ½ cups boiling water
2 (11 oz.) cans mandarin oranges, drained
1 (8 oz.) can diced peaches, with juice
1 (6 oz.) can frozen orange juice concentrate, thawed
1 (3.5 oz.) pkg. instant vanilla pudding mix
1 (8 oz.) pkg. cream cheese, softened
1 cup milk

Spray a 9x13 inch pan with cooking oil. Combine gelatin and boiling water, stirring until dissolved. Add mandarin oranges, peaches and orange juice. Transfer to pan and chill in refrigerator until firm. Beat together pudding mix, cream cheese and milk. Spread over gelatin and refrigerate until chilled.

Baked Cinnamon Apples

6 Granny Smith apples, cored and peeled around top rim of each apple
cinnamon, to taste
nutmeg, to taste
6 teaspoons organic Sucanat
3 teaspoons unsalted butter

Preheat oven to 350 degrees. Place apples in a Pyrex™ dish and top each with ½ teaspoon of butter, dash of cinnamon and nutmeg, and Sucanet. Bake for 45 minutes. Serve warm.

Excerpted from Healthy Foods: an irreverent guide to understanding nutrition and feeding your family well by Leanne Ely (ISBN 1-891400-20-7)

> NOTE FROM THE RUSH HOUR™ COOK: Just so I don't break my own rule—Sucanat stands for Sugar Cane Natural. This is a healthy substitute for sugar and you can find it at natural food stores.

You-Choose-the-Chip Cookies

Makes about 2 dozen

1½ cups butter, melted
2 cups sugar
2 eggs
1 teaspoon vanilla extract
2 cups flour
¾ cup unsweetened cocoa powder
1 teaspoon baking soda
½ teaspoon salt
2 cups chips of your choice—peanut butter, chocolate or use M&M®s

Preheat oven to 350 degrees. Mix butter and sugar in a large bowl. Beat in eggs and vanilla. In a separate bowl combine flour, cocoa, baking soda, and salt and gradually stir into the butter mixture. Mix in chips. Drop by rounded teaspoons onto ungreased cookie sheets. Bake 8 to 10 minutes. Let set for 2 minutes and then transfer to wire racks to cool completely.

Chocolate Dipped Strawberries

Strawberries (as many as you like!)
semi-sweet chocolate chips (the more the better!)

In double boiler (or pan set in a hot water bath) <u>gently</u> melt semi-sweet chocolate bits until smooth, stirring constantly.

Clean large strawberries and pat dry. Leave stems on for "handles." Dip your large strawberries, half way up, in the melted chocolate.

Cool on a tray lined with wax paper until chocolate is set. Store in refrigerator.

FAMILY FAVORITES

Cinnamon Streusel Coffee Cake

1 egg
¼ cup sugar
1 cup skim milk
2½ cups low-fat Bisquick™
2 tablespoons butter

Streusel:
1 cup brown sugar, firmly packed
2 tablespoons ground cinnamon
2 teaspoons nutmeg
¼ cup butter, melted
1 cup sugar

Combine ingredients for streusel mixture and set aside. To prepare coffee cake, beat egg, sugar and milk on low speed with an electric mixer. Add Bisquick™ and melted butter and beat until blended on low speed. Add ½ of streusel mixture, stirring just until blended. Sprinkle ½ of remaining streusel mixture over bottom of greased pan. Pour in ½ of batter creating an inner circle of streusel within batter. Pour remaining batter over top. Bake for 20 to 25 minutes or until a knife inserted in center comes out clean.

Excerpted from: 365 Quick, Easy and Inexpensive Dinner Menus by Penny E. Stone (ISBN 1-891400-33-9, www.championpress.com)

Snicker™ Bar Salad

3 Granny Smith apples, chopped
3 red delicious apples, chopped
1 standard bag 'fun size' Snicker™ bars, diced
1 large container of whipped topping
1 cup of mini marshmallows
Coconut or cashews (optional)

Dice apples and Snickers™ into small pieces and fold into the whipped topping. Fold in mini-marshmallows. Store in refrigerator. Top with a sprinkle of shredded coconut or cashews (optional).

Your Personal Shopper

As the former Queen of Non-Cooking Excuses, one of those I used most often was that I just didn't have enough time to get organized, plan and get everything from the store. To avoid the same excuse-ridden fate in your future, I am including Your Personal Shopper right in this cookbook. You have three different five-day menus to choose from. You'll find a grocery list for each of those meal plans as well.

Personal Shopper List #1

Your Five-Day Menu:
1. Make Mine a Melt (35) *serve* with Potato Shapes (16)
2. Christmas Eve Chili (38) with French Bread
3. Sammy's Favorite Noodle Bake (41) serve with breadsticks and tossed salad
4. Tantalizing Taco Salad (26)
5. Pasta Presto (29)

Meats:
- ☐ 2.5 lb ham, shave or thinly slice 1 pound, cube the rest
- ☐ 3 lb. lean ground beef
- ☐ 1lb. turkey

Produce:
- ☐ 3 cups chopped bell pepper (any color will do just fine)
- ☐ 3 tomatoes
- ☐ 2 heads romaine lettuce
- ☐ 3 garlic cloves
- ☐ 1 medium onion
- ☐ handful of mushrooms
- ☐ 1 bunch green onions (optional)

Dry and Canned Goods:
- ☐ 9 ounces angel hair pasta (or any other pasta)
- ☐ 1 10-oz. jar of Alfredo Sauce (I like the one that is made by Five Brothers™)
- ☐ 1 jar spaghetti sauce
- ☐ 1 package penne pasta
- ☐ 1 can tomato paste
- ☐ 2 (14.5 oz.) cans diced tomatoes (preferably a spicy Mexican style)

Dairy:
- ☐ 12 oz. of cheddar cheese
- ☐ 3 garlic cloves
- ☐ margarine or butter

- ☐ sour cream (if desired)
- ☐ 1 container fat-free ricotta
- ☐ 1 bag part-skim mozzarella cheese
- ☐ Parmesan cheese

Frozen:
- ☐ 3 cups broccoli florets

Spice List:
- ☐ salt and pepper
- ☐ cumin
- ☐ chili powder
- ☐ oregano and basil
- ☐ Cajun spice mix
- ☐ Worcestershire
- ☐ rosemary

Other Stuff:
- ☐ red wine (optional for chili)
- ☐ beer (optional for chili)
- ☐ beef broth (optional for chili)
- ☐ coffee (optional for chili)
- ☐ 3 Hershey kisses™ (optional for chili)
- ☐ small bag of baked tortilla chips
- ☐ 2½ cups bottled salsa, you choose the heat
- ☐ loaf of French bread or bagels
- ☐ sugar or brown sugar
- ☐ Italian bread sticks
- ☐ cooking spray

Add your own items:

_____

_____

_____

_____

_____

Personal Shopper List #2

Your Five-Day Menu:
1. Let-me-Soak Chicken (28) serve with Sugar Carrots (17)
2. Cheesy Scalloped Spuds (21)
3. Tasty Tortellini Soup (20) with Potato and Broccoli Bake (24)
4. Ultra Quick Chicken and Rice (42)
5. The Super Stack (36) with Quick Chips (20) and Spastic Salsa (17)

Meats:
- ½ pound deli-sliced ham
- ½ pound deli-sliced turkey
- 16 chicken breasts (Alter this number to meet your family needs. It is currently set for 6 Servings. If you need to serve more or less than 6, take the number of people to serve, multiply by two and then add four—this is the number of chicken breasts you should purchase.

Produce:
- 1 large bag carrots
- 1 Jalapeno Pepper
- 3 cups broccoli florets
- 2.5 lb bag of potatoes
- 1 lemon
- cauliflower

Dry and Canned Goods:
- 1 (14.5 oz.) can diced tomatoes
- 1½ cups chicken broth
- 1 (10¾ oz.) can cream of chicken soup
- 1½ cups instant rice
- 1 small can tomato paste
- 1 (10¾ oz.) can cream of mushroom soup
- jarred sauce
- 1 (14.5 oz.) can mex-style corn
- taco seasoning mix

Dairy:

- ☐ 7 oz. package refrigerated tortellini
- ☐ 1¾ cups reduced-fat cheddar cheese
- ☐ 1 cup milk
- ☐ margarine or butter
- ☐ ½ cup part-skim mozzarella cheese
- ☐ 8 oz. fat-free sour cream
- ☐ 12 slices of Alpine Lace cheese
- ☐ ½ cup low-fat Ricotta cheese

Frozen:
- ☐ 2 cups frozen peas

Spice List:
- ☐ salt and pepper
- ☐ basil
- ☐ 1 packet of taco seasoning mix
- ☐ Rosemary
- ☐ red pepper

Other Stuff:
- ☐ 7 flour tortillas
- ☐ olive oil or Italian fat-free dressing
- ☐ 6 slices bread
- ☐ bread crumbs
- ☐ brown sugar
- ☐ sugar
- ☐ spray cooking oil

Add your own items:

_____
_____
_____
_____

Personal Shopper List #3

Your Five Day Menu:
1. Must-Have Meatloaf (53) serve with Quickslaw (22)
2. Mexi-Casserole (48)
3. "Pizza Pockets" (46) serve with Snicker™ Bar Salad (62)
4. Parmesan Pasta Bowl (27) serve with French bread and whipped unsalted butter
5. Fine Fettuccini (50) serve with French bread and whipped unsalted butter

Meats:
- ☐ 18 oz. chicken breast, diced
- ☐ 1 pound ground beef (or turkey)
- ☐ 1 pound ground turkey

Produce:
- ☐ 2 cups cabbage, shredded
- ☐ 1 cup carrots, shredded
- ☐ 1⅓ cups chopped onion
- ☐ 10 garlic cloves
- ☐ 3 Granny Smith apples
- ☐ 3 red delicious apples

Dry & Canned Goods:
- ☐ 2 cups orzo (rice shaped pasta)
- ☐ 1 cup mini marshmallows
- ☐ ¾ cup Italian breadcrumbs
- ☐ 8 oz. tomato sauce
- ☐ 6 oz. elbow macaroni
- ☐ 3 (14.5 oz.) cans diced tomatoes
- ☐ 12 oz. canned corn
- ☐ 20 oz. canned chicken broth
- ☐ 4 oz. pizza sauce
- ☐ 12 oz. fettuccini noodles

Dairy:
- ☐ ½ cup Parmesan, freshly grated
- ☐ 1 egg

- ☐ ½ cup part-skim mozzarella cheese
- ☐ ½ cup fat free half and half
- ☐ 1 small container whipped unsalted butter
- ☐ 1 (10 oz. package) refrigerated pizza crust

Frozen:
- ☐ 1 large container whipped topping
- ☐ 1½ cups frozen peas

Spice List:
- ☐ salt and pepper
- ☐ 2 packets of taco seasoning mix
- ☐ ketchup
- ☐ garlic salt

Other Stuff:
- ☐ 1 cup mayonnaise (I use fat free)
- ☐ your choice of pizza toppings
- ☐ 2 tablespoons flour
- ☐ white wine
- ☐ olive oil
- ☐ ¼ cup sugar
- ☐ 1 standard bag 'fun size' Snicker™ Bars
- ☐ 2 loaves French bread
- ☐ shredded coconut (optional)
- ☐ cashews (optional)

Add your own items:

_____

_____

_____

_____

_____

_____

THE RUSH HOUR COOK

EFFORTLESS ENTERTAINING
by Brook Noel

THE TALES AND RECIPES OF A CORPORATE WOMAN TACKLING TODAY'S KITCHEN

CHAMPION PRESS LTD.

MILWAUKEE, WISCONSIN

Dedication

This book is dedicated to my mom, who has always been there to answer life's tough questions...

"Mom... I'm trying to cook a recipe and it calls for 3 cups cooked chicken. How exactly do I cook the chicken?"

You're the best ... I love you!

Contents

IN THE BEGINNING...
AWESOME APPETIZERS

Broiled Melbas	14
Pizza Petites	14
Beef Bowl	15
The Versatile Deviled Egg	16
Cinnamon Chips	16
Chicken Spirals	18
Chili Cheese Dip	19
Caramel Dip	19
Zucchini Corn Salsa	20
Spinach Dip Surprise	20
Cal-Zoned Out	21
Picken Chicken	22
Mushroom Stuffed Crescent Roll-Ups	22
Fly Away Chicken Wings	23
Guacamole	24
Everyone's Favorite Party Meatballs	24
Sauerkraut-Free Reuben Appetizers	25
Ravishing Roasted Veggies	26
Aunt Sally's Potatoes	26
Can't Have A Party Without Me French Onion Soup	27
Divine Dressings	28
Quick Vinaigrette	28
Orange-Vinegar Dressing	28
Honey-Dijon Dressing	28
Sweet-Sour Dressing	28
Lemon-Garlic Vinaigrette	28
Balsamic Vinaigrette	29
Potato and Bacon Soup	29

A MERRY MIDDLE...
ENTICING ENTREES

Chicken Enchiladas	32
Quick-To-Mix, Long-To-Cook Italian Roast	32
Tex-Mex Madness	33
One Package Fits All	35
Beef Roast With Onion-	

Mushroom Gravy	35
Perfect Parmesan Chicken	36
Guide's Pie	36
Magnificent Mac	37
Non-Boring Beans	37
Caribbean Chicken	38
It's a Wrap	39
Pizzalad	39
Chicken With Mushroom-Sherry Sauce	40
Kids-Love-It Casserole	40
Italian Chicken In A Flash	41
Sloppy Joes	41
Fun And Fresh Fish Sticks	42
Turkey Parmesan	42
Sara's Super Magnificent Pasta & Meatballs	43
Beef Fajitas	44
Filet Mignon With Perfect Peppercorn Sauce	45
Garlic Sauce Option	45
Stroganoff Supper	46
Chicken Stew	47

A Sweet & Happy Ending... Delectable Desserts

It's A Miracle Cake	50
Perfect Pistachio Torte	51
Tantalizing Tarts	51
The Best Bread Pudding	52
Minute Meringue Dessert	52
Debi's Million Dollar Chocolate Chip Cookies	53
Summer Melon a la Mode	54
Fondue For You	54
Vanilla Berry Dream	54
Cinnamon & Spice Make Everything Nice	55
No Bake Turtle-Brownie Fudge Sundae	55
Simple Strawberry Shortcake	56
Snicker® Bar Surprise	56
Fluffy Fruit	57
Pan Fried Bananas	57

Etcetera...

A Few Things You'll Need to Know	7
The Birth of the Rush Hour Cook™	9
The Five Rules	12
Entertaining Basket	15
Simple Centerpieces	15
Preparation & Presentation Primer	18
Did It Good	20
Mind Your Mouthful	22
Get Crazy with Croutons	24
Tips for Divine Dressing	29
Excuses, Excuses	34
Delight in Diverse Dishes	44
The Basics of Wine	47
Entertaining Guidelines	50
Rush Hour™ Cleaning Tip	53
Entertaining Checklist	58
Personal Shopper – List # 1	60
Personal Shopper – List # 2	62
Personal Shopper – List # 3	64

A Few Things You'll Need to Know...

Pay close attention when you see this symbol. It means that you are about to uncover a 'Mother-Knows-Best' tip which will save you countless headaches when feeding your children.

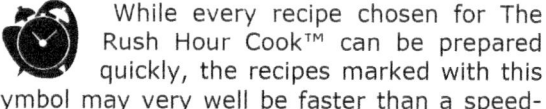

While every recipe chosen for The Rush Hour Cook™ can be prepared quickly, the recipes marked with this symbol may very well be faster than a speeding bullet. I've also used this symbol to denote recipes that save valuable time or offer make-ahead options.

At the end of this book, you'll find a section called, Your Personal Shopper. I've included pre-planned menus and grocery lists to get you through those rough weeks when you don't feel like planning - which is just about every week, for me! These are the recipes that I now use much to my family's satisfaction and success.

Serve It Up—All recipes are sized for 6 Servings, unless otherwise noted. If you have a family of 3 or 4, consider adding a few more members or better yet, make the full recipe anyway. Use the rest for lunches the following day, or freeze these extras as healthy, homemade options to those ready-made, chemical-laden convenience-meals.

High-fat, some-fat, low-fat or no-fat—Most of the recipes within this book are either low in fat or easily adaptable for low fat options. When prepared this way, the caloric and fat intakes in each meal contain less than 30% fat.

Make Your Misto™— In most cookbooks, almost every recipe calls for cooking spray. Instead of using the aerosol cans that you can buy in the store, purchase a Misto™ or other non-aerosol pump. With these pumps, you can add a bit of olive, canola or vegetable oil and they will convert the oil to spray. This allows you to use the minimum amount of oil and avoid the nasty-chemicals found in their store-shelved counter-parts.

Introduction:
The Birth of Effortless Entertaining

Me? Entertain? I stared at my friend across the table—surely she had lost her mind. Through *The Rush Hour Cook's™ Family Favorites* cookbook I had just taken my first innocent and wobbly steps into the world of cooking. Now she had the nerve to suggest another book—**entertaining!**

Those of you familiar with the first book in *The Rush Hour Cook™ Series* know that I could also be called The Queen of Non-Domesticity. Upon occasion, I have gone as far as converting my stove to extra shelving space. Warning: if you do this, make sure to leave a note on the front of the stove indicating such, or you could be in for a nasty surprise when your significant other (or visiting family member) presumes the stove is used for cooking. Just ask my husband, who has been interrupted one too many times by the smoke alarm, to appreciate my handy storage shortage solution.

In any event, you get the picture—the kitchen is not my refuge. To me the kitchen is more like a little square room, with machinery that is waiting to turn on you at any minute—burning, hardening or otherwise ruining carefully labored over fare. My longing for the return of the family dinner forced me to face this fear and make a deal with my appliances. I wouldn't use them as furniture if they would quit making my food taste less than par. The results of my struggle to find family-friendly, quick and affordable, meals with common ingredients is detailed in *The Rush Hour Cook™: Family Favorites,* along with shopping lists and other tips to transform the frenzied and frightful household dinner hour into a smooth and sane dining experience.

But entertaining? I had a hard enough time trying to dye Easter eggs with my daughter and her seven-year-old girlfriend last week!

We were going to dye Easter eggs after dinner. The first hurdle came when I read the instructions on the PAAS® dye. I shuddered in horror while two young, hopeful and expectant girls stared at me. Vinegar? I made a quick dash back to the market. The way everything comes in a boxed kit these days, one would figure they could include a vinegar packet! After returning from the store and properly mixing my dye, we were ready to begin. It was nearing 9:00 P.M. on a school night, but I had promised we would color eggs—and so be it, we would. I would have made Martha proud! I was ready—over 12 colors of dye and 6 dozen eggs waiting in the wings.

"Whatchya doing?" Samantha's friend Cassie asked curiously, as I carried the eggs to the table.

"Getting our eggs," I replied excitedly.

"Arentchya gonna cook them?" she asked again.

"Oh….. of course, I was—I mean, I am." I did a quick 180 degree turn, grabbed a pan of water and tossed it on the stove. I reached for *Betty Crocker's* advice on preparing hardboiled eggs.

Don't get me wrong—it's not that I am antisocial. Just because I convert every formal dining room we have into a library, craft room or play room doesn't mean that I wouldn't enjoy company. I relish the thought of families mingling over perfectly cut, crustless, tea-sized sandwiches and layered salads while sipping punch made with juice from freshly squeezed fruit. But here's the thing—I relish the thought of it at, *someone else's* house! In order to actually do this at *my* house—a few things would need to happen. First, people like to mingle when they entertain, which means they would have to be able to walk throughout the house without risk of injury from scattered toys. If I could even fathom corralling all the toys back into their master's room I'm sure I'd discover floors and countertops in my home. But then I'd have to clean and organize those very countertops and floors!

My last and biggest hang-up is that most people expect to eat when they are entertained. Personally, I'm a bit intimidated by the word appetizer—not to mention when you start throwing entrée, main course, etc. into the equation. When I look at the food spreads on television, in cookbooks and in magazines, it looks like there must have been at least 8 years lead time for the food preparation. Who has that kind of attention time anymore?

Truth be told—I'd love to have friends over more often—whether it be formal or informal. In order to do that I would need an arsenal of realistic recipes for the person who wants to entertain—but doesn't have 100 hours (or a staff of 12) to execute the preparation.

"Exactly," said my friend. "You could find the recipes that could really work for practical, everyday entertaining."

As much as I had never thought of myself as a cookbook writer, I realized this book would give me some time to enjoy with friends as I used them as "guinea pigs" during my recipe testing. (Not to mention, it would also force me to clean up.)

As always, I feel it's important to stay focused when working on any book and I have found that setting a few rules and criteria for recipe selection truly helped the process.

The rules for my entertaining recipes remain the same as my original Rush Hour Cook™ rules...

The Five Rules of Rush Hour Recipes:

1. All ingredients should be able to be pronounced accurately through the phonetic use of the English Language.

2. Each ingredient can be located in the market without engaging in a full scale scavenger hunt.

3. No list of ingredients shall be longer than the instructions.

4. Each recipe has to be durable enough to survive me, the Queen-of-Incapable-Cooking, and elicit a compliment at meal's end.

5. My finicky child will eat it—or some portion of it. I've learned not to be too picky on this one. Often I separate out part of the meal during preparation and customize it to her taste.

So without further adieu, I'm off to my "kitchen-sentence". By the time you read this, I will have discovered many new recipes that work (and 10 times as many that didn't) and hopefully just as many special memories of cherished times entertaining friends and family. I hope you'll do the same!

Brook Noel
The Rush Hour Cook™

IN THE BEGINNING...
Awesome Appetizers

In the Beginning: Awesome Appetizers

Broiled Melbas	14
Pizza Petites	14
Beef Bowl	15
The Versatile Deviled Egg	16
Cinnamon Chips	16
Chicken Spirals	18
Chili Cheese Dip	19
Caramel Dip	19
Zucchini Corn Salsa	20
Spinach Dip Surprise	20
Cal-Zoned Out	21
Picken Chicken	22
Mushroom Stuffed Crescent Roll-Ups	22
Fly Away Chicken Wings	23
Guacamole	24
Everyone's Favorite Party Meatballs	24
Sauerkraut-Free Reuben Appetizers	25
Ravishing Roasted Veggies	26
Aunt Sally's Potatoes	26
Can't Have A Party Without Me French Onion Soup	27
Divine Dressings	28
Quick Vinaigrette	28
Orange-Vinegar Dressing	28
Honey-Dijon Dressing	28
Sweet-Sour Dressing	28
Lemon-Garlic Vinaigrette	28
Balsamic Vinaigrette	29
Potato and Bacon Soup	29

EFFORTLESS ENTERTAINING

Broiled Melbas
Makes 30 melba treats

1 cup light mayonnaise
1 cup freshly grated Parmesan cheese
1 teaspoon parsley
30 melba round crackers

Combine mayo and Parmesan cheese. Add parsley. Spread a teaspoonful onto each melba round and broil, in single layer, on a cookie sheet until golden brown (1-2 minutes). There is plenty of room for variation on this recipe. Be creative in choosing your toppings. Try cheddar cheese and bacon bits, Swiss cheese and chives, American cheese and ham...let each family member "make a combo" and then do taste tests to select the "Melba King (or Queen".

Pizza Petites
Makes 25-30 pizza squares

½ teaspoon dried parsley
¼ cup diced green onions
½ cup reduced-fat cream cheese
½ teaspoon oregano
½ teaspoon dried basil
12 inch Italian bread shell
1 cup sliced green pepper
1 cup sliced red pepper
Parmesan Cheese

Mix parsley, green onion, cream cheese and herbs. Spread over a 12 inch Italian bread shell. Top with green onions, peppers and Parmesan. Bake until heated through. Cut into squares and serve with toothpicks.

If many children will be present when you entertain consider making an extra batch of these pizza treats. If a child doesn't like the main course or other appetizers, Pizza Petites have good odds!

Beef Bowl

1 lb. lean ground beef
½ teaspoon cumin
¼ teaspoon pepper
½ cup salsa
bread bowl (or chips)
sour cream (optional)

Brown beef in a frying pan over medium heat. Drain off fat. Add cumin and pepper. Stir in ½ cup salsa or enough to moisten the beef. Simmer on low heat for five minutes. Transfer mixture to the inside of a bread bowl and serve with bread pieces on the side. Or transfer into a bowl and serve with chips and sour cream.

Simple Centerpieces

Mix a tad of creativity and a splash of style and what do you get? A simple and inexpensive centerpiece! Try one of these easy ideas to decorate your next spread.

~ For birthday parties or holiday celebrations, display festively wrapped packages at the table's center. For Christmas celebrations display glass ball ornaments in an attractive basket, or fill empty glass balls with potpourri and a "good wish" handwritten on a small piece of paper. Let each guest take an ornament home.

~ Place pretty rocks or marbles in a charger or other shallow dish. Add pillar candles of different heights nestled into the marbles.

~ Purchase "odds and ends" napkins with pretty patterns. Wrap silverware in colored napkins and place in a lined basket.

~ Use nature as your inspiration and fill a charger or other shallow dish with a display of nature's offerings. Some ideas: pinecones, wildflowers, pine boughs, beach glass, etc.

The Versatile Deviled Egg
Makes 7 servings

7 hard boiled eggs, halved
¼ cup mayonnaise
¼ cup sour cream

Remove yolks and mash. Stir in mayonnaise, sour cream and one of the following:

4 tablespoons sun dried tomatoes, finely chopped
3 tablespoons capers, finely chopped
4 tablespoons cooked bacon, crumbled
4 tablespoons smoked salmon, mashed

Fill the halves with the mashed yolk mixture. Top each egg with one of the following:
green or black olive
parsley
chives
Parmesan cheese
paprika

Cinnamon Chips
Sweeten your next spread with these easy-to-prepare chips.

6 flour tortillas
5 tablespoons melted butter
cinnamon and sugar

Cut flour tortillas into 8 pieces, making triangular chips. Spread the chips on a cookie sheet in a single layer. Drizzle butter evenly over chips. Sprinkle with cinnamon and sugar. Bake in a 350 degree oven for 10-12 minutes. Let cool and then transfer to a serving dish.

Preparation & Presentation Primer

While I wish I could say I was innovative enough to come up with these guidelines on my own—no one would believe me anyway. Many of these simple rules come from my mother and my aunt's legacy. Others I pressured out of good friends in the catering business.

Breaking New Ground – Only 20% of your recipes should be "new" recipes. Make sure that you have cooked everything else at least one time before, so that you feel confident in serving your guests. This way if one of your "new" recipes doesn't work, you know you have a back up of recipes that will be enjoyed.

Make A List and Check it Twice – It takes only a few minutes to fill out a planning checklist and this process alone removes 80% of the stress from the thought of entertaining. Try using the planning worksheet included at the back of this book.

Prepare as much of the food as you can beforehand - When choosing your dishes, remember that the more work you do beforehand the less stress entertaining will bring. Try to keep the recipes that require complete preparation the day of entertaining to two or three.

Cook with Contrast – Vary your recipes by color, texture and temperature for a more appealing display. For example, use contrasting colors or try a few crunchy and a few smooth choices. Create a balanced mix of hot and cold dishes.

Chicken Spirals

Makes 8 servings

4 chicken breasts, halved
8 slices of deli ham
4 slices of Swiss cheese
1 cup broccoli florets, cooked
⅛ teaspoon pepper
1 beaten egg white
1 tablespoon water
1 cup bread crumbs

Place each chicken breast half between 2 pieces of waxed paper. Pound lightly to an ⅛" thickness. Remove plastic wrap. Fill with ham, Swiss cheese and broccoli evenly between the four chicken breasts. Fold in long sides of chicken and roll into a spiral. Secure with toothpicks

In a bowl, mix egg white and water. In a separate dish, mix bread crumbs and seasonings. Dip the chicken in egg white then bread crumbs to coat evenly. Transfer spirals into a baking dish, coated with cooking oil.

Bake in a 400 degree oven for 20 to 25 minutes or until chicken is tender and no longer pink. Remove toothpicks. Slice and display over fresh greens on a serving platter.

Make-Ahead Tip: Prepare this recipe all the way up to the baking. Instead of placing it in the oven, place it in the refrigerator. It can sit for up to 10 hours. Cook a little longer if dish is placed cold into the oven.

If your child is as finicky as mine, the site of "green" in her food equals, "I don't like it." In that case, prepare a portion of the spirals without broccoli.

Chili Cheese Dip

Makes 8 servings

1 can Hormel™ chili without beans
1 package (16 oz.) Velveeta™ cheese
corn or tortilla chips, for dipping

Maybe not the beacon of health... but it doesn't get much easier than this! (Besides, when you are entertaining, no one can read the label!) Put chili and cheese in a crockpot on medium heat. Stir occasionally until melted. Serve! Spice lovers can add red pepper sauce to taste.

Caramel Dip

caramel candies (soft, chewy kind)
apples

Melt caramel candies over low heat. Core and quarter apples for dipping. For variety, purchase one or two of each apple type carried by your local market.

Consider serving this as a dessert instead of ice cream.

Dip It Good!

Forget those boring old plastic containers and colored bowls—bring on the peppers! Try this creative display to brighten up your table.

Cut the tops off green, yellow and red bell peppers and scoop out seeds and ribbing. Place dips inside. You can also carve the top off a small pumpkin, remove seeds and ribbing, and fill with a favorite dip.

Zucchini Corn Salsa

1 medium red onion, finely chopped
1 tablespoon sugar
1 cup red wine vinegar
1 teaspoon salt
1 teaspoon pepper
1 medium zucchini, scrubbed and diced
1 cup canned, frozen or fresh corn
1 teaspoon olive oil

Combine onion, sugar and vinegar and marinate for 30 minutes. Drain off vinegar. Set aside. Sauté zucchini until soft, set aside. Toss all with remaining ingredients.
Serve chilled or warm.

Spinach Dip Surprise

Makes 8 servings

1 (10 oz.) package frozen chopped spinach, drained
1 package dry vegetable soup mix (I like Mrs. Grass™)
1 (8 oz.) container sour cream
1 cup mayonnaise
1 (8 oz.) can water chestnuts, chopped
1 round rye bread or sourdough bread to make "bread bowl."

Mix all ingredients and chill for one hour. Serve in hollowed out round rye or sourdough bread. Tear up hollowed out bread for dipping.

DON'T LET A SMALL KITCHEN STOP YOU FROM ENTERTAINING...INSTEAD, GET CREATIVE! PULL OUT DRAWERS AND COVER THEM WITH CUTTING BOARDS OR SLATS OF WOOD COVERED WITH WAX PAPER. TRY AN IRONING BOARD TOPPED WITH A TABLE CLOTH FOR EXTRA COUNTER OR BUFFET SPACE.

Cal-Zoned Out

Makes 8 servings

1 tube refrigerated crescent rolls
¼ cup pizza sauce
½ teaspoon garlic
¼ teaspoon basil
½ teaspoon oregano
1(8 oz.) package of mozzarella cheese
2 tablespoons melted butter
Parmesan cheese, grated

Fill according to your taste, such as:
   pepperoni
   pre-cooked Italian sausage
   onion
   green pepper
   black olives
   pineapple
   Canadian bacon
   Roma tomatoes

Open can of crescent rolls and separate. Fill with desired items. Fold into triangles and pinch edges shut, to form pouches. Bake for 12 to 15 minutes at 375 degrees. When done immediately brush with melted butter and sprinkle with Parmesan cheese or Italian seasoning. Serve with extra pizza sauce for dipping. A great dish to make-ahead and freeze in individual Ziploc® bags.

Mind Your Mouth(fuls)

Curious to know how many appetizers per person to prepare? Here are the average eating habits of partygoers:

Party without a main meal 12-15 mouthfuls
Meal included, 6-8 mouthfuls

Picken Chicken

1 pound pre-cut chicken breast strips
1 onion, chopped
1 green pepper, chopped
1 teaspoon chili powder
1 teaspoon red pepper flakes
1 teaspoon fresh garlic (or garlic powder)
¾ cup salsa
1 package flour tortillas cut in half

Sauté onion and green pepper until soft. Set aside. Using the same pan, stir-fry chicken until no longer pink. Add chili powder, red pepper flakes and garlic. Add back onion and green pepper. Simmer to blend. Just before serving, add salsa. Serve warm with tortillas.

Mushroom Stuffed Crescent Roll-Ups

1 tube of refrigerated crescent rolls
1 (4 oz.) can of mushrooms
1 bunch of fresh chives, minced
½ cup Parmesan, blue or Feta cheese
1 teaspoon garlic

Sauté mushrooms, chives and garlic for 2-3 minutes. Roll out crescent rolls and place a dollop of the mushroom mixture in the center of each crescent roll. Sprinkle cheese choice on mixture and roll into crescent shapes. Bake 2-5 minutes longer than the crescent roll directions for perfectly cooked roll-ups.

Fly Away Chicken Wings

Makes 8 servings

4 pounds chicken wings or drummies
½ cup butter or margarine, melted
½ cup hot pepper sauce
½ teaspoon red pepper
1 teaspoon lemon juice, optional
carrots and celery, cut into julienne strips
Blue Cheese or ranch dressing
1 Reynolds™ cooking bag

Cut wings into three pieces discarding the wing tips (no meat in there). Combine butter, hot pepper sauce, red pepper and lemon juice in Reynolds™ bag and shake to combine the ingredients. Add the wings and shake again, coating well. Bake in preheated 425 degree oven for 45-50 minutes. Remove to a platter and serve with veggies and blue cheese or ranch dressing, for dipping

For a child's portion go easy on the spices and definitely opt for ranch dressing over Blue Cheese.

Get Crazy with Croutons

Forget the standard, boring store-bought croutons. Using small cookie cutters, cut shapes out of sliced bread. Lightly coat a frying pan with oil and cook the shapes until golden. Toss on salads and soups!

Guacamole
Makes 8 servings

2 ripe avocados (should be soft to the touch but firm)
1 tablespoon garlic powder
2 tablespoons of your favorite salsa
a dash of lemon juice
chips or veggies

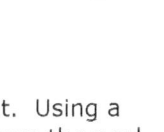

Cut avocado in half. Remove pit. Using a spoon, scoop out the avocado from the peel. Place into a small serving bowl. Mash with a fork. Mix in garlic powder and salsa. Mix in a dash of lemon juice. Viola! Or should I say Ole'!

Everyone's Favorite Party Meatballs
Makes 5 dozen

1 pound ground beef
½ cup dry, commercial breadcrumbs
⅓ cup finely chopped onion
1 tablespoon parsley
1 teaspoon salt
1 teaspoon Worcestershire sauce
½ teaspoon pepper
1 egg
1 (12 oz.) bottle chili sauce
1 (10 oz.) jar grape jelly

Mix ground beef, breadcrumbs, onion, parsley, salt, Worcestershire sauce, pepper and egg together. Shape into 1-inch meatballs. Brown meatballs in skillet over medium heat, about 10 minutes, turning frequently. Drain off fat. Pour chili sauce and jelly over meatballs and stir constantly until the jelly has melted. Place in crockpot and simmer until guests arrive. This recipe is best if the meatballs have at least 1 hour to simmer.

Sauerkraut-Free Reuben Appetizers

Makes 8 servings

1 pound deli prepared ham salad
1 package (8 oz.) shredded Swiss or mozzarella cheese
1 package square cocktail rye bread slices

Heat oven to 400 degrees. Place rye bread slices on cookie sheet. Top with ham salad and shredded cheese. Bake 10 minutes or until cheese is melted. Serve immediately.

Useless Yet Interesting Trivia

The first pretzel was purportedly made in 600 A.D. by a monk in Northern Italy. During the Lenten season he was unable to use any milk, fat or eggs. When the monk used flour, water and salt, he came up with "pretzel" dough. He formed the dough into the shape of two arms crossed in prayer. Originally, he named it "pretiola" which is Latin for "Little gift."

Ravishing Roasted Veggies

1 cup zucchini
1 cup carrots
1 cup broccoli
1 cup cauliflower
1 cup onion
1 cup green pepper
1 cup yellow squash
¼ cup olive oil
2 tablespoons red wine vinegar (optional)
2 tablespoons minced garlic
1 teaspoon salt
1 tablespoon pepper
1 tablespoon oregano

Preheat oven to 375 degrees. Cut vegetables into bite sized pieces. Mix olive oil, red wine vinegar (optional), garlic, salt, pepper and oregano together. Toss with vegetables. Bake for 20 minutes. Stir. Bake another 20 minutes or until veggies are tender.

Aunt Sally's Potatoes

Makes 8 servings

1 red onion sliced
1 (32 oz.) package of frozen hashbrowns
1 (8 oz.) container of sour cream
1 (8 oz.) package of shredded cheddar cheese
1 (10¾ oz.) can cream of chicken soup, undiluted
2 tablespoons butter
1 teaspoon garlic powder
salt and pepper to taste
1 can of Durkees™ fried onions

Preheat oven to 350 degrees. Mix all ingredients together except fried onions and place in a casserole dish. Bake covered for 60 minutes. Let stand for 15 minutes. Top with fried onions and bake for an additional 10-15 minutes, uncovered, until browned and bubbly.

Can't Have a Party Without Me French-Onion Soup

Makes 9 servings

2 tablespoons butter
3 onions, sliced thinly and separated into rings
½ teaspoon sugar
½ teaspoon black pepper
3 tablespoons flour
4 (14.5 oz.) cans beef broth
1 (10.5 oz.) can beef consommé
½ cup dry white wine
2 teaspoons Worcestershire sauce
9 slices of French bread, toasted
9 slices of mozzarella or Gruyere cheese

Melt butter in Dutch oven. Cook onions over medium heat until transparent. Add all except the last two ingredients. Stir well and simmer for at least 30 minutes, more if desired. Scoop into bowls and top with a piece of French bread and cheese. Broil until cheese melts.

Entertaining Basket

If you plan on having visitors on a regular basis, create an Entertaining Basket. Keep all your basic supplies here for easy finding. You might want to include tent cards, plasticware and extra napkins and, of course, a copy of this book.

EFFORTLESS ENTERTAINING

Divine Dressings

Containers:
Rinse out store-bought dressing bottles when empty along with other jars with tight-fitting lids. These make perfect "shakers" for dressing. For quick vinaigrette try...

Quick Vinaigrette

Three parts oil to one part vinegar or four parts oil to one part lemon juice.

Use an almost-empty dressing jar as the basis for a delightfully Dijon dressing! Below are a few for you to try....

Orange Vinegar Dressing

Try adding equal parts orange juice and white wine vinegar—then a dash of olive oil to an almost empty Dijon-mustard container. Shake well. The dressing will keep for 7 days.

Honey Dijon Dressing

Mix 1 part honey to one part orange juice—add mustard to flavor. Shake well.

Here are some more fun combos to try...

Sweet & Sour Dressing

2 tablespoons honey
2 teaspoons Dijon-style mustard
½ cup unsweetened apple juice
salt and pepper to taste
Blend ingredients, shaking well.

Lemon-Garlic Vinaigrette

¼ tsp. dry mustard
⅓ cup extra-virgin olive oil
2 tablespoons lemon juice
2 tablespoons red wine vinegar
1 clove minced garlic
Place in a jar and shake well. Makes 8 servings.

Balsamic Vinaigrette

½ cup balsamic vinegar
⅓ cup extra-virgin olive oil
1 tablespoon sugar
*excerpted from *Cooking for Blondes* by Rhonda Levitch. ISBN 1-891400-80-0
www.championpress.com

Potato and Bacon Soup

Makes 12 servings

4 pounds baking potatoes
5 slices of bacon
3 cups onion, chopped
1 teaspoon salt
5 garlic cloves, minced
6 cups milk
1 teaspoon black pepper
3 cups chicken broth
1 cup sliced green onion
1 cup cheddar cheese, shredded

Bake potatoes in microwave or 400 degree oven. Once tender, mash the potatoes just a bit, leaving skins on. Set aside. Cook bacon in a large skillet until crisp. Remove bacon and drain on paper towel. Crumble bacon and add to potatoes. Add onion to pan and sauté 5 minutes. Add salt, pepper and garlic and sauté another two minutes. Add broth, potatoes and milk, and bring to a boil. Reduce heat and simmer for 8-12 minutes. Ladle into bowls and top with green onions and cheese.

A MERRY MIDDLE...
Main Meals in Minutes

Quick Recipe Index:

Chicken Enchiladas	32
Quick-To-Mix, Long-To-Cook Italian Roast	32
Tex-Mex Madness	33
One Package Fits All	35
Beef Roast With Onion-Mushroom Gravy	35
Perfect Parmesan Chicken	36
Guide's Pie	36
Magnificent Mac	37
Caribbean Chicken	38
It's a Wrap	39
Pizzalad	39
Chicken With Mushroom-Sherry Sauce	40
Kids-Love-It Casserole	40
Italian Chicken In A Flash	41
Sloppy Joes	41
Fun And Fresh Fish Sticks	42
Turkey Parmesan	42
Sara's Super Magnificent Pasta & Meatballs	43
Beef Fajitas	44
Filet Mignon With Perfect Peppercorn Sauce	45
Garlic Sauce Option	45
Stroganoff Supper	46
Chicken Stew	47

EFFORTLESS ENTERTAINING

Chicken Enchiladas

1 package Louis Rich™ southwest chicken strips
1 onion, chopped
1 (8 oz.) jar roasted red pepper, chopped
1 teaspoon cumin
1 teaspoon garlic powder
1 teaspoon hot sauce
1 (8 oz.) package of Mexican grated cheese
1 (10 oz.) can enchilada sauce
12 corn tortillas

Preheat oven to 375 degrees. Cook onion until soft. Add red pepper and seasonings to onion. Sauté for 2 minutes. Add chicken to mixture. Simmer for 5 minutes. Set filling aside. Pour ½ can of enchilada sauce into a 9x13 inch baking dish. Put approximately ⅓ cup of filling into each tortilla. Roll tortillas and put seam side down in dish. Cover with remaining sauce and sprinkle with cheese. Bake 15-20 minutes or until cheese has melted and the sauce bubbles.

Make a child-friendly version with just chicken strips and cheese wrapped in the tortilla. Top with enchilada sauce if desired.

Quick-to-Mix, Long-to-Cook, Italian Roast

Makes 8 servings

3 pound beef round roast
1 onion, sliced
2 garlic cloves, minced
½ teaspoon each—salt and pepper
1 (8 oz.) can tomato sauce
1 package Italian salad dressing mix

Place onion in bottom of crockpot. Add roast. Top with remain ingredients. Cover and cook on high setting for 5 hours or until meat is tender.

Tex-Mex Madness

Makes 5 servings

1 pound lean beef, diced
1 cup shredded taco cheese
5 cups tomatoes, chopped
1 cup salsa
3 cloves garlic
1 tablespoon chili powder
5 cups instant white rice, cooked and set aside

Sauté beef for 2-3 minutes over medium-high heat. Add ½ cup of cheese and the rest of ingredients except rice. Simmer until vegetables are tender—about 5 minutes. Spoon over cooked rice and top with remaining cheese.

Excuses... Excuses...

Looking for a reason to throw a party? You don't need to look far. Here are a few of my favorites:

1. Your boss gets fired.
2. Your child has their first "on the pot" experience.
3. Your mother-in-law is going to visit someone *else* this summer.
4. You got a new blender.
5. You have all kinds of food in your fridge which you will never eat by yourself, if you want to fit into your shorts this year.
6. You found out your ex-boyfriend, a.k.a. the love of your life, has been divorced and remarried three times and gained 50 pounds and is unemployed.
7. You learned how to reset the clock and timer on both your microwave oven and VCR.
8. Your child ate four bites of vegetables without a 15 minute preamble on human torture.
9. You got something fixed before the warranty expired.
10. The price of gasoline dropped more than a nickel.

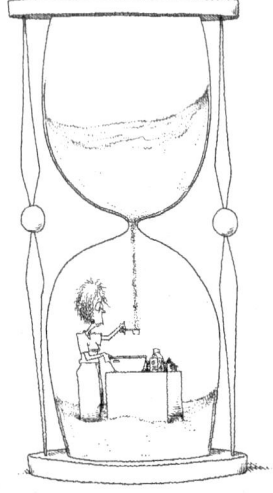

FUSSY EATERS? GUESTS WITH DIFFERENT TASTES OR NUTRITIONAL REQUIREMENTS?

One Package Fits All

2-3 pounds cooked meat cut up (chicken, beef, ham, shrimp)
assorted chopped veggies (onions, green pepper, corn, broccoli, potatoes, carrots, zucchini)
1 can cream of mushroom soup
assorted sauces (barbecue, teriyaki, balsamic vinegar, etc.)
1 cup water
spices (salt, pepper, garlic, red pepper flakes, oregano)
aluminum foil sheets (12x18) for each guest

Keep all items refrigerated until ready to use. Add one tablespoon of water and one tablespoon cream of mushroom soup to each foil packet. Have each guest fill their packet with ingredients and seal shut. Pierce packet with different colored toothpicks for each guest. Bake in preheated oven at 450 degrees for 18 to 22 minutes. Serve with a green salad and French bread.

Beef Roast with Onion-Mushroom Gravy

3 to 4 pound beef roast, trimmed of excess fat
1 envelope Lipton™ dry onion soup mix
2 tablespoons A-1 Sauce™
2 cans cream of mushroom soup
1 soup can water
1 teaspoon salt
1 onion, chopped
2 cups fresh sliced mushrooms

Place roast in crockpot. In a separate container, combine dry onion soup mix with A-1 sauce™, cream of mushroom soup, water, salt, chopped onion and sliced mushrooms. Pour over meat. Cover with lid and cook on high for

7-9 hours. *Excerpted from: Crazy About Crockpots! By Penny E Stone www.championpress.com*

Perfect Parmesan Chicken

Makes 4 servings

4 boneless, skinless chicken breasts
¾ cup Miracle Whip™
1 cup bread crumbs
½ cup Parmesan cheese
1 teaspoon salt
1 tablespoon pepper
1 tablespoon oregano

Preheat oven to 350 degrees. Mix crumbs, cheese, salt, pepper and oregano. Brush chicken with Miracle Whip™ and coat with crumb mixture. Bake in a 9 x 13 inch baking dish for 45 minutes or until golden brown.

Guide's Pie

1 pound ground beef or turkey
⅛ cup red wine vinegar
2½ cups beef broth
33 oz. prepared mashed potatoes, (instant is my choice!)
¼ cup horseradish
2 tablespoons cornstarch
1½ cups frozen peas
1½ cup cheddar cheese

Preheat oven to broiling. Brown meat with vinegar and 1 cup broth. Drain off any fat. Set aside. Mix horseradish and cheddar cheese into mashed potatoes and set aside. Mix cornstarch, remaining broth and peas in a small sauce pan and heat 'til thickened to form a gravy. Mound meat mixture in center of broiler proof pan. Surround with mashed potatoes. Pour gravy over center. To finish, broil 7-10 minutes, or until potatoes are lightly browned and dish is thoroughly heated.

Magnificent Mac

If you are expecting kids at your get-together, I guarantee a serving of this magnificent mac will tame the troops.

3 cups chicken broth
1½ cups skim milk
¾ pound elbow macaroni
1½ tablespoons cornstarch
1½ cups frozen peas
½ pound Canadian bacon, cubed
8 oz. cheddar cheese, shredded

In a large sauce pan or Dutch oven bring broth, milk and macaroni to a boil. Cook for 10 minutes, stirring frequently. Blend cornstarch with 5 tablespoons of water. Stir into pan and continue stirring until mixture returns to a boil. Add peas and bacon; mix well and then remove from heat. Add cheese and stir for 1-2 more minutes, to incorporate.

Non-Boring Beans

3 cups cooked green beans
2 tablespoons crushed garlic
¼ cup bacon, cooked and crumbled
1 tomato, diced

Cook beans as usual. Drain and toss with other ingredients for a quick party dish.

Caribbean Chicken

5 cloves garlic, pressed
2 Jalapeno peppers, seeded and chopped (use gloves)
⅜ cup lemon juice
¼ cup honey
2 teaspoons thyme
6 boneless, skinless chicken breasts

Mix all ingredients, except chicken, together in a blender. Pour prepared marinade and chicken into a large Ziploc® plastic bag. Turn chicken around several times to coat with marinade. Refrigerate at least 2 hours, but no longer than 6 hours.

For the best flavor, grill chicken on the barby, turning and brushing frequently with marinade, until the juice of chicken is no longer pink when thickest pieces are cut. Discard any remaining marinade—that's a food poisoning waiting to happen! Don't you go drenching your hot cooked chicken in that stuff for "more flavor". You'll make yourself sick! If your grill is covered with snow, use your oven. Preheat to 375 degrees and cook about 45 minutes or until chicken is no longer pink.

Excerpted from: The Frantic Family Cookbook by Leanne Ely, C.N.C.(ISBN 1-891400-11-8 www.championpress.com)

Odd Invites

Add some spice to your next party by asking each person that you invite to bring a dish that starts with the same letter as their last name.

It's A Wrap

6 flour tortillas
mayonnaise
6 strips crisp bacon
½ pound turkey
½ pound ham
6 slices American cheese
1 tomato, sliced
shredded lettuce
1 red onion sliced, optional
toothpicks

Spread mayo on tortillas. Top with lettuce, onion, tomato and meat. Add cheese and then roll up and secure with two toothpicks. Cut in half and serve with your favorite chips or sides.

IT'S A PIZZA... IT'S A SALAD... IT'S A...
Pizzalad

1 tube refrigerated pizza dough
1 (8 oz.) package Mozzarella cheese
1 packaged Caesar salad mix
24 slices pepperoni
Parmesan cheese, freshly grated

(Hint-if you are adventurous and like pesto, spread pre-made pesto on the crust before adding the cheese)

Preheat oven to 425 degrees. Grease cookie sheet and roll out pizza dough onto cookie sheet. Bake for 12 minutes. While the crust is cooking, mix Caesar salad according to the package. Top crust with mozzarella cheese and bake until cheese is melted, approximately 5 to 7 minutes more. Allow to cool for 10 minutes. Cut into six pieces and serve topped with salad mix and four pepperoni slices. Garnish with freshly grated Parmesan cheese.

EFFORTLESS ENTERTAINING

Chicken with Mushroom-Sherry Sauce

6 boneless, skinless chicken breasts
1 cup flour
2 tablespoons olive oil
1 tablespoon butter or margarine
1 (7 oz.) can of mushrooms
dash of cooking sherry
1 teaspoon Worcestershire sauce
1 tablespoon crushed garlic
½ diced onion
1 cup chicken broth

Wash chicken breasts in cold water and dredge in flour (the flour will help thicken your sauce). Over low heat, add olive oil and butter to the pan. Gently sauté onion and garlic and push to the edge of the pan. Place the floured chicken breasts in the center of the pan and sauté each side till golden brown, about 10 minutes. After the chicken is browned, stir in mushrooms, cooking sherry, Worcestershire sauce and broth. While stirring, loosen all the good browned bits in the pan. Cover and simmer 30 minutes or until the chicken breasts are done, adding more broth or water as needed. Serve with mashed potatoes and roasted vegetables, or your favorite rice dish.

Kids-Love-It Casserole

1 pound ground beef
1 (15 oz.) can chunky tomato sauce
1 can refrigerated pizza crust dough
1 ½ cup mozzarella cheese, shredded

Cook meat until browned. Add sauce and cook until heated through. Meanwhile, press pizza dough into a 9 x 13 baking dish. Sprinkle ½ cup of cheese over dough. Add meat mixture. Bake in a 425 degree oven for 10-15 minutes. Add remaining cheese and bake an additional 5 minutes or until cheese is melted.

Four simple ingredients...kids love it... could it get any easier?

Can you tell I love Chicken?

Italian Chicken in a Flash

1 cup Italian dressing
6 chicken breast halves
Parmesan cheese
olive oil

Pound halved chicken breasts to ¼ inch thickness. Marinate with Italian dressing for at least 15 minutes (preferably an hour). Sauté in olive oil over medium heat until the chicken juices run clear, approximately 12-15 minutes. Serve with your favorite buttered pasta or roasted vegetables.

Another sane and simple four-ingredient recipe.

Sloppy Joes

1 pound lean ground beef
1 oz. can tomato sauce
1 tablespoon Worcestershire sauce
1 green pepper, diced
1 yellow onion, diced
1 teaspoon salt
¼ teaspoon pepper
1 teaspoon Italian seasoning
1 teaspoon dried oregano
1 teaspoon dried sweet basil
⅛ teaspoon garlic powder

Brown ground beef in a skillet with onion and green pepper. Drain off all grease. Stir in tomato sauce, Worcestershire sauce and all other seasonings. Simmer over low heat for 10 minutes. Serve on either bread or buns.

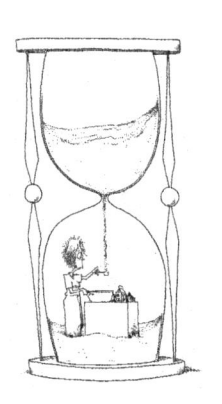

Excerpted from: 365 Quick, Easy and Inexpensive Dinner Menus by Penny E Stone (ISBN 1-891400-33-9, www.championpress.com)

Fun and Fresh Fish Sticks
Makes 4 servings

1 pound cod fillets
½ cup Italian seasoned bread crumbs
¼ cup Parmesan cheese
1 tablespoon pepper
1 tablespoon parsley
½ teaspoon paprika
¼ tablespoon garlic salt
½ cup buttermilk
2 cup all-purpose flour
1 lemon, sliced
tartar sauce, pre-made from store

Preheat oven to 425 degrees. Cut fillets into ¾ inch strips; set aside. You will need 3 shallow bowls. Place seasonings (breadcrumbs, cheese, pepper, parsley, paprika and garlic salt) in one bowl; buttermilk in the second bowl and the flour in the third. Coat fish with flour first, buttermilk second and seasonings last. Place on greased cookie sheet and bake for 15-20 minutes until golden brown and fish flakes easily. Serve with lemon slices and tartar sauce. Can be made as an appetizer or served as a main dish with roasted potatoes and coleslaw.

Turkey Parmesan
3 pounds turkey cutlets
¾ cup Italian-seasoned coating
1½ cup pasta sauce
1 cup Parmesan cheese, shredded
olive oil

Place turkey between two sheets of waxed paper and flatten with rolling pin. Coat with Italian-seasoned coating. Heat oil over medium-high heat. Cook cutlets 2 minutes per side or until done. Transfer cutlets to serving dish. Heat sauce in microwave and pour over cutlets. Top with Parmesan cheese.

Sara's Super Magnificent Pasta and Meatballs

Makes 8 servings

1 (16 oz.) package mini penne pasta
1 pound ground beef
1 egg
½ cup Italian bread crumbs
1 tablespoon oregano
1 teaspoon basil
1 teaspoon black pepper
2 tablespoons chopped minced garlic
1 tablespoon dry minced onion
1 jar spaghetti sauce (I like Classic™ Italian sausage with peppers and onions)
1 (7 oz.) can mushrooms or 8 ounces fresh mushrooms
Parmesan cheese

Prepare water according to package directions for pasta. Mix ground beef, breadcrumbs, egg and spices together in mixing bowl with hands. Heat frying pan sprayed with cooking spray or 1 tablespoon oil over medium heat. Roll meat mixture into 1-inch balls. Cook until browned and cooked all the way through. Add spaghetti sauce and mushrooms to meatballs and simmer over low heat. Cook pasta. Rinse pasta after cooking. Pour sauce and meatballs over pasta in a serving dish. Top with grated Parmesan cheese.

(Hint-if you like spice, you can use Tabasco™ garlic pepper sauce. Add it to the sauce and at the table. If you don't have time to make the meatballs, substitute cooked Italian sausage.

Beef Fajitas

1 pound lean boneless beef, cut into ¼-inch strips
1 teaspoon cumin
1 teaspoon chili powder
½ teaspoon pepper
1 green bell pepper, seeded and sliced
1 cup onion, sliced
¼ cup lime juice
12 (6-inch) flour tortillas
2 cups shredded lettuce
2 cups reduced-fat cheddar cheese, grated
1 cup salsa

Slice onion and green pepper. Cut raw meat into ¼ inch slices. Store in refrigerator until ready to use. Sprinkle beef on all sides with cumin, chili powder and black pepper. Spray large skillet with cooking oil. Heat. Add beef, bell pepper and onion; cook over high heat stirring constantly until beef is no longer pink. Add lime juice; toss to combine. Warm tortillas in microwave if desired. To assemble fajitas, place an equal amount of beef mixture onto center of each tortilla, top with ¼ cup lettuce and equal amount of cheese, and 2 tablespoons salsa. Roll tortillas to enclose filling.

Excepted from: *Frozen Assets Lite & Easy* by Deborah Taylor-Hough.(ISBN 1-89140-019-3, www.championpress.com)

Delight in Diverse Dishes

Don't get bent out of shape if you don't have enough plates and dishes of one style for serving your guests... simply mix and match! Varying patterns makes a more colorful and rich display. You may even enjoy starting a collection of favorite patterns. This also allows you to find great deals on "odds and ends" dishes!

Filet Mignon with Perfect Peppercorn Sauce

6 beef filets
1 teaspoon cracked black pepper
½ cup onion, minced
½ cup bourbon
1 cup beef broth
¼ cup Dijon Mustard
½ teaspoon salt

Sprinkle steaks with salt and black pepper. Cook steaks five minutes on each side over medium-high heat or to desired doneness. Remove steaks and keep warm. Add remaining ingredients to pan and stir well. Reduce heat and cook for 2-4 minutes, stirring constantly. Top steaks with sauce and serve immediately.

For kids offer Ketchup as a sauce! Although ketchup will not make your child a connoisseur of exquisite tastes—it does dramatically increase the odds of food consumption when incorporated as a food group offered almost daily.

Garlic-Sauce Option:

You can change the taste of this dish dramatically by adjusting the sauce. Here is another one of my favorites:

2 teaspoons thyme
½ teaspoon salt
½ teaspoon pepper
12 garlic cloves, unpeeled
½ cup beef broth

Broil garlic for 5-7 minutes. Cut off bottom of each clove and squeeze innards into a blender or food processor. Add remaining ingredients and blend until smooth. Warm in the microwave for 30-60 seconds and serve over steaks, as above.

> When serving a buffet of food, vary the heights of the dishes for a more bountiful-looking spread. Fan food for flair.

Stroganoff Supper
Makes 8 servings

button mushrooms, to equal 1½ cups, sliced
2 pounds beef tenderloin, cut into strips
1 cup beef broth
1 cup chicken broth
1 cup dry white wine
½ cup sour cream
2 tablespoons unsalted butter
1 cup onion, minced
3 tablespoons brown sugar
2 tablespoons flour
egg noodles cooked
cooking oil

Heat oil in a large skillet over medium-high heat. Sauté mushrooms for 3-5 minutes or until lightly browned. Transfer mushrooms to bowl. Place beef strips in pan. Cook for 2-3 minutes per side and then add to mushrooms in bowl. Add beef broth to pan. Simmer until reduced to ¼ cup. Add onion, brown sugar and flour. Gradually add chicken broth, sour cream and wine. Simmer over low heat until sauce is well blended. Return mushrooms and beef to pan and heat through. Serve over noodles.

* Make a double or triple batch and store remaining in freezer containers for a quick and easy meal later! To reheat, simply place in refrigerator before going to work. That night, while fresh egg noodles are cooking, pour mixture into a saucepan and warm over low to medium heat. If too thick, add a bit of chicken broth.

Chicken Stew

Makes 8 servings

2 pounds boneless chicken breasts, cut into bite-size pieces
1 onion, chopped
1 cup celery, chopped
4 cloves garlic, minced
3 cans chicken broth
1 cup water
8 oz. egg noodles
1½ cup frozen mixed vegetables
1½ cup frozen peas
1½ cup frozen carrots

In large saucepan cook chicken, onion and garlic for 5 minutes with a bit of oil. Add celery, chicken broth and water. Cover and simmer for 15 minutes. Add frozen vegetables and egg noodles and simmer uncovered until noodles are tender. Serve with French bread.

The Basics of Wine

Forget worrying about flavor, sniffing, breathing and all that jazz. Use the simple guide below for quick and easy wine pairings.

APPETIZERS – Serve white or sparkling wines. Dry sherry is also a good choice.

FISH DISHES – Serve crisp white wines.

PASTA DISHES – Serve robust red wines.

MEAT DISHES – For beef choose a merlot or cabernet. For chicken and pork, you can't go wrong with a chardonnay.

DESSERTS – Offer a port wine or a fruitier wine such as a Chianti.

A Sweet & Happy Ending...

Delectable Desserts

Quick Recipe Index:

It's A Miracle Cake	50
Perfect Pistachio Torte	51
Tantalizing Tarts	51
The Best Bread Pudding	52
Minute Meringue Dessert	52
Debi's Million Dollar Chocolate Chip Cookies	53
Summer Melon a la Mode	54
Fondue For You	54
Vanilla Berry Dream	54
Cinnamon & Spice Make Everything Nice	55
No Bake Turtle-Brownie Fudge Sundae	55
Simple Strawberry Shortcake	56
Snicker™ Bar Surprise	56
Fluffy Fruit	57
Pan Fried Bananas	57

It's a Miracle Cake!

Makes 12 servings

2 cups flour
1 cup sugar
3 tablespoons cocoa
2 teaspoons baking soda
½ teaspoon salt
1 cup water
1 cup Miracle Whip™
½ package chocolate chips (6 oz.)
½ cup of brown sugar, packed

Preheat oven to 375 degrees. Mix flour, sugar, cocoa, baking soda and salt. Add water and Miracle Whip™ gradually to dry ingredients. Pour batter into a 9x13 pan and sprinkle with chocolate chips and brown sugar. Bake for 30 minutes or until a toothpick inserted in the middle comes out clean. No frosting required!

Entertaining Guidelines Gathered from the Pros:

Although I may not be an "A-Rated Entertainer", I have quite a few friends who are. Here are their tips and tricks.

Choose variations and contrasting foods. For example, serve a balance of hot and cold foods, textures and colors.

Vary your timing by selecting a few recipes that can be made-ahead with those that need last minute attention.

Make sure to check your dishes and serving utensils prior to the party to ensure you have everything you need in stock.

Think disposable! Disposable dishes, plastic ware, etc. can really lighten your entertaining load and clean up.

Perfect Pistachio Torte

2 cups or 1 sleeve graham crackers, crushed
6 tablespoons butter or margarine melted
¼ cup sugar
1 cup crushed pecans
2 cups cold milk
2 packages (4 serving size) pistachio instant pudding, be sure to use instant
1 (8 oz.) tub whipped topping, thawed

Mix graham crackers, butter, sugar and ½ of the pecans. Press firmly into bottom of a 9 x 13 pan. Pour milk and pudding mixes into a large mixing bowl. Beat two minutes or until well blended. Put ½ of the pudding into the graham cracker crust. Mix remaining pudding with ½ of the whipped topping. Spread on top of pudding already in crust, making a second layer. Top with remaining whipped topping. Sprinkle with remaining pecans. Chill for 4 hours or until set.

Tantalizing Tarts

6 tablespoons preserves (any flavor you like)
1 (3.5 oz.) vanilla pudding cup
6 mini graham cracker piecrusts (Keebler™ makes these)
1 cup sliced fruit—you choose the type (strawberries, blackberries, blueberries, raspberries or kiwi)

Spoon 2 tablespoons of pudding into each tart crust. Top with fruit. Heat preserves in a microwave on high setting until melted for about a minute. Spoon a bit of preserves over each tart. Let set 10 minutes before serving. Simple to make and very impressive looking!

The Best Bread Pudding

Makes 12 servings

6 eggs, beaten well
1 cup sugar
2 cups light cream
1 stick butter or margarine, melted
1 tablespoon vanilla
1 large French bread torn into pieces
1 teaspoon nutmeg
1 teaspoon cinnamon
1 teaspoon allspice
1 cup raisins, soaked in hot water for 15
   minutes and drained

Preheat oven to 350 degrees. Grease 9x13 inch pan. Beat eggs with sugar, cream, butter and vanilla. Place bread cubes in pan. Pour egg mixture over the bread. Coat bread cubes well with mixture. Add nutmeg, cinnamon, allspice and raisins to the mixture, stirring well. Bake for 30 to 40 minutes or until the pudding is set. Serve warm with whipped cream.

Minute Meringue Dessert

6 store-bought baked meringues
   (unless you're Martha—then bake them
   yourself. Of course, if you're Martha, you
   probably aren't reading this book.)
3 cups chocolate, vanilla or strawberry frozen
   nonfat yogurt
1½ cups strawberries, sliced
chocolate syrup
whipped topping

Scoop ½ cup of frozen yogurt into each meringue. Top with ¼ cup strawberries, 1 tablespoon of chocolate syrup and a dollop of whipped topping.

Debi's Million Dollar Chocolate Chip Cookies

Makes 10 dozen

(Seem like a lot? You'll be thankful after you try one! These are freezer friendly so you can keep a stash for later. Store a dozen per bag and freeze.)

2 cups butter
2 cups sugar
2 cups brown sugar
4 eggs
2 teaspoons vanilla
1 teaspoon salt
2 teaspoons baking powder
2 teaspoons soda
4 cups flour
5 cups blended oatmeal*
2 (4 oz.) chocolate chips
1 (8 oz.) chocolate bar(grated)
3 cups chopped walnuts

*First, measure oatmeal. Then blend into a fine powder in a mill or blender.

Cream together butter and both sugars. Add eggs and vanilla. Sift together and then stir in salt, baking powder, baking soda and flour. Stir in blended oats. Mix in chips, grated chocolate bar and nuts. Roll into balls, and place two inches apart on cookie sheet. Bake 10 minutes at 375 degrees.

Excerpted from: Frozen Assets by Deborah Taylor-Hough (ISBN 1-891400-61-4, www.championpress.com)

Rush Hour Cleaning Tip

No time to clean? Give your abode a quick touch-up by thinking silver! Grab the Windex™ and wipe down all silver faucets, doorknobs, mirrors, etc. You'll be amazed what a little sparkle will do!

Summer Melon a la Mode
Makes 4-6 servings

1 cantaloupe
ice cream, frozen yogurt or sherbet
coconut or mint (optional)

Cut a cantaloupe (or honeydew) into 4 to 6 wedges. Place a generous scoop of vanilla ice cream (or frozen yogurt or sherbet) in the center. Sprinkle with freshly grated coconut or garnish with a sprig of mint (optional).

Fondue for You
2 (14 oz) cans condensed milk
1 cup semi-sweet chocolate chips

Combine milk and chocolate over low heat until melted.

Serve as a dipping sauce for:
strawberries
graham crackers
bananas
marshmallows
cantaloupe
angel food cake
lady fingers

Vanilla Berry Dream
Makes 4 servings

1 package instant vanilla pudding
2 cups cold milk
2 cups mixed fresh berries (raspberries, blueberries, strawberries)
whipped topping

Mix pudding with milk in bowl. Beat with wire whisk or electric mixer on lowest speed 2 minutes. Pour into 4 dessert cups or bowls. Refrigerate for at least 30 minutes until set. Top with berries and cool whip. Serve well chilled.

Cinnamon & Spice Make Everything Nice

Makes 8 servings

1 (8 oz.) can of refrigerated crescent style dinner rolls
1 tablespoon margarine or butter, melted
2 tablespoons sugar
1 teaspoon cinnamon
1 teaspoon nutmeg
powdered sugar

Preheat oven to 375 degrees. Spray cookie sheet with oil. Unroll dough and separate triangles. Cut triangles in half to form two smaller triangles. Mix sugar, cinnamon and nutmeg. Brush triangles with melted butter. Sprinkle sugar, cinnamon and nutmeg over triangles. Roll into a crescent shape. Brush tops with remaining butter and sprinkle with remaining sugar mix. Bake at 375 degrees for 9 to 13 minutes. Top with powdered sugar after removing from oven. Serve.

No Bake Turtle-Brownie Fudge Sundae

Makes 8 servings

8 brownies from your local bakery or grocery store bakery
vanilla custard or ice cream
Smuckers™ hot caramel topping
Smuckers™ hot fudge topping
whole pecans
whipped cream

Put brownies into serving dish. Top with rest of the ingredients in the order listed. Kids will love to choose what topping and build their sundae. Serve! Substitute strawberry topping for the caramel.

EFFORTLESS ENTERTAINING

Simple Strawberry Shortcake
Makes 8 servings

1 angel food cake cut into 8 pieces
1 (16 oz.) package fresh strawberries
½ cup sugar
whipped topping

Wash and hull strawberries (or if you are like me, just cut the top off). Slice strawberries. Place in container and mix with sugar. Cover and refrigerate for at least two hours. Mix once while chilling. Place strawberries and juice from the strawberries on top of the angel food cake. Top with whipped cream and chocolate syrup, if desired.

Snicker® Bar Surprise
Makes 8 servings

2 Snickers® candy bars sliced into ½ inch
  pieces or 8 fun size bars cut into thirds
2 sliced red delicious apples
2 sliced green apples
1 (12 oz) container whipped topping
cocktail peanuts
chocolate and caramel sauce (optional)

Combine Snickers®, apples and whipped topping in a serving bowl. Top with remaining whipped topping. Sprinkle with cocktail peanuts and drizzle with chocolate and caramel sauce if desired.

Fluffy Fruit

Makes 8 servings

1 dozen egg whites
2 envelopes Knox™ unflavored gelatin
1 cup fresh blueberries
1 cup fresh strawberries
1 cup fresh raspberries or blackberries

Beat egg whites and gelatin until stiff peaks form. Semi-mash fresh berries with sugar to taste. Fold into egg white mixture. Freeze until set. Garnish with a few whole berries and sprigs of mint.

Pan Fried Bananas

3 bananas, cut into thick slices
2 tablespoons butter
1 tablespoon brown juice
2 tablespoons orange juice
1 tablespoon rum

Sauté thickly sliced bananas in brown sugar and butter for two minutes. Sprinkle with orange juice and rum.

Skip rum when preparing for children.

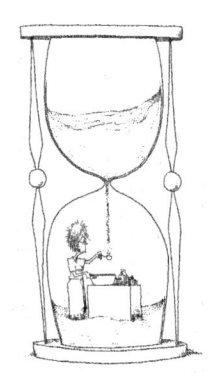

Entertaining Checklist

Planning for a party? Use this prep guide to make your planning run smoothly.

One month prior	Choose site and party theme (It's much easier to decide on invites and menus with a theme.) Draw up the guest list and menu.
3 weeks before	Make your shopping list. Check your recipes to see what you can make-ahead of party day.
2 weeks before	Order any decorations or extras—cakes, flowers, etc.
1 week before	Order any food that is needed. Decide on table setting and gather up tablecloths, serving ware, etc.
5 days before	Confirm your guest list and decide on seating arrangements.
4 days before	Do your shopping. Find one or two friends to come early on party day to help with last-minute items.
3 days before	Prepare any make-ahead items. Check to make sure you have all the serving utensils, platters and pots needed for the party day.
2 days before	Set table. Make and place guest cards.
1 day before	Set up all food that can be set up and cover with plastic wrap until party day. Pick up any ordered items.
Morning of party	Do last minute prep and hot foods.

Your Personal Shopper

As the former Queen of Non-Cooking Excuses, one of those I used most often was that I just didn't have enough time to get organized, plan and get everything from the store. To avoid the same excuse-ridden fate in your future, I am including Your Personal Shopper right in this cookbook. You have three different five-day menus to choose from. You'll find a grocery list for each of those meal plans as well.

Your Personal Shopping List # 1

Your Five-Day Menu:
1. Kids-Love-It Casserole (40) served with Chicken Spirals(19)
2. Super Stroganoff Supper (46) served with Snicker™ Bar Surprise (56)
3. Quick-To-Mix, Long-To-Cook Italian Roast (32) served with Minute Meringue Dessert (52)
4. Pizzalad (39) served with Simple Strawberry Shortcake (56)
5. Perfect Parmesan Chicken (36) served with Potato and Bacon Soup (28) Perfect Pistachio Torte (51)

Meats
- ☐ 1 lb. ground beef
- ☐ 3 lbs. beef round roast
- ☐ 24 slices pepperoni
- ☐ 8 chicken breasts
- ☐ 8 slices of deli ham
- ☐ 5 slices of bacon
- ☐ 2 lbs. beef tenderloin

Produce
- ☐ 3½ cups strawberries
- ☐ 1 pkg. Caesar salad mix
- ☐ 1 cup broccoli florets
- ☐ 4 lbs. baking potatoes
- ☐ 5 onions
- ☐ 7 garlic cloves
- ☐ 1 green onion
- ☐ 1½ cups button mushrooms
- ☐ 2 green apples
- ☐ 2 red delicious apples

Dry and Canned Goods
- ☐ 15 oz. can chunky tomato sauce
- ☐ 8 oz. tomato sauce
- ☐ 2 cups bread crumbs
- ☐ 3 cups chicken broth

- ☐ 1 cup beef broth
- ☐ 1 pkg. egg noodles
- ☐ 2 pkgs. (4 serving size) pistachio instant pudding

Dairy
- ☐ 1 lb. unsalted butter
- ☐ 4 slices Swiss cheese
- ☐ 1 cup Cheddar cheese
- ☐ 1 can Parmesan cheese
- ☐ 1 egg
- ☐ 1 gallon milk
- ☐ ½ cup sour cream

Frozen
- ☐ 1 chocolate frozen nonfat yogurt
- ☐ 2 (12 oz.) whipped topping

Spice List
- ☐ salt and pepper
- ☐ oregano
- ☐ ¾ cup Miracle Whip™
- ☐ 1 pkg. Italian salad dressing mix

Other Stuff
- ☐ 1 tablespoon water
- ☐ chocolate syrup
- ☐ caramel sauce
- ☐ 1 angel food cake
- ☐ 6 baked meringues
- ☐ 2 cans refrigerated pizza crust dough
- ☐ cooking oil
- ☐ 1 cup dry white wine
- ☐ brown sugar
- ☐ flour
- ☐ graham crackers
- ☐ sugar
- ☐ 1 can pecans
- ☐ 2 Snicker™ candy bars

Add Your Own Items:

Your Personal Shopping List # 2

Your Five-Day Menu:
1. Caribbean Chicken (38) served with Fluffy Fruit(57)
2. Kids-Love-It Casserole (40) served with Debi's Million Dollar Chocolate Chip Cookies (53)
3. Filet Mignon with Perfect Pepper corn Sauce (45) served with Zucchini Corn Salsa (21)
4. Italian Chicken in a Flash (41) served with Summer Melon a la Mode (54)
5. Beef Bowl (15) served with Simple Strawberry Shortcake (56)

Meats
- ☐ 12 boneless, skinless chicken breasts
- ☐ 2 lb. ground beef
- ☐ 6 beef filets

Produce
- ☐ ½ cup onions
- ☐ 1 red onion
- ☐ 2 jalapeno peppers
- ☐ 1 cup blueberries
- ☐ 1 cup strawberries
- ☐ 1 cup raspberries or blackberries

Dry and Canned Goods
- ☐ 1 (15 oz.) chunky tomato sauce
- ☐ 1 cup Italian dressing
- ☐ beef broth
- ☐ Dijon Mustard
- ☐ coconut
- ☐ mint
- ☐ white vinegar
- ☐ **sugar**
- ☐ brown sugar
- ☐ olive oil

Dairy
- [ ] sour cream
- [ ] whipped topping
- [ ] 1 dozen egg whites
- [ ] 1 can refrigerated pizza crust dough
- [ ] 1½ cup mozzarella cheese
- [ ] butter
- [ ] 4 eggs
- [ ] Parmesan cheese

Frozen
- [ ] ice cream, frozen yogurt or sherbet
- [ ] 1 cup corn

Spice List
- [ ] cumin
- [ ] garlic
- [ ] thyme
- [ ] vanilla
- [ ] salt and pepper
- [ ] cracked black pepper
- [ ] baking powder
- [ ] baking soda

Other Stuff
- [ ] lemon juice
- [ ] honey
- [ ] Knox™ gelatin
- [ ] bourbon
- [ ] coconut
- [ ] 1 angel food cake
- [ ] flour
- [ ] oatmeal
- [ ] chocolate chips
- [ ] walnuts

Add Your Own Items:

_____

_____

_____

_____

_____

Your Personal Shopping List # 3

Your Five-Day Menu:
1. Tex-Mex Madness (33) served with Vanilla Berry Dream (54)
2. Turkey Parmesan (42) served with It's a Miracle Cake (50)
3. Magnificent Mac (37) served with Minute Meringue Dessert (52)
4. Quick-To-Mix, Long-To-Cook, Italian Roast (32) served with The Versatile Deviled Egg (17)
5. Guides Pie (36) served with No Bake Turtle Brownie Fudge Sundae (55)

Meats
- [ ] 1 lb. diced lean beef
- [ ] 3 lb. turkey cutlet
- [ ] Canadian bacon
- [ ] 1-3 lb. Beef round roast
- [ ] 1 lb. ground beef or turkey

Produce
- [ ] 5 cups tomatoes, chopped
- [ ] garlic
- [ ] 2 cups mixed berries
- [ ] 1 onion
- [ ] 1½ cup strawberries

Dry and Canned Goods
- [ ] instant potatoes (33 oz.)
- [ ] 5 cups instant rice
- [ ] 1 pkg. instant vanilla pudding
- [ ] 1½ cups pasta sauce
- [ ] 1 cup Miracle Whip™
- [ ] 3 cups chicken broth
- [ ] ¾ lb. macaroni
- [ ] ¼ c mayonnaise
- [ ] 1 (8 oz.) can tomato sauce
- [ ] 1 pkg. Italian dressing mix
- [ ] 2½ cups beef broth

Dairy

- [ ] cheddar cheese
- [ ] shredded taco cheese
- [ ] milk
- [ ] whipped topping
- [ ] Parmesan cheese
- [ ] skim milk
- [ ] 7 hard boiled eggs
- [ ] sour cream

Frozen

- [ ] 3 cups peas
- [ ] vanilla custard or ice cream
- [ ] chocolate, vanilla or strawberry frozen nonfat yogurt

Spice List

- [ ] corn starch
- [ ] chili pepper
- [ ] Italian seasoning
- [ ] Cocoa powder
- [ ] salt and pepper
- [ ] baking soda

Other Stuff

- [ ] red wine vinegar
- [ ] salsa
- [ ] olive oil
- [ ] 8 store bought brownies
- [ ] chocolate syrup
- [ ] 6 store bought meringue shells
- [ ] Smuckers™ hot fudge topping
- [ ] Smuckers™ hot caramel topping
- [ ] chocolate chips
- [ ] brown sugar
- [ ] flour
- [ ] sugar

Add Your Own Items:

THE RUSH HOUR COOK

ONE-POT WONDERS
by Brook Noel

THE TALES AND RECIPES OF A
CORPORATE WOMAN TACKLING
TODAY'S KITCHEN

CHAMPION PRESS LTD.
Milwaukee, Wisconsin

Dedication

For Mindy-thanks for all your encouragement, dedication and faith!

Contents

In the Beginning...
Awesome Appetizers

Pizza Dip	14
Apple Dip	14
Choose-A-Way-Breadsticks	15
Denise's Pizza Wheels	16
Aztec Salad	16
Party Pinwheels	17
Spicy Salsa	17
Join The Club Salad	18
Pretzel Dip	18
Baked Mozzarella Sticks	19
I Slaved All Day Cheddar and Herb Biscuits	20
Cheesy Potato Soup	20
Grecian Style Potatoes	21
Chicken Tortilla Soup	22

A Merry Middle...
Main Meals in Minutes

Way Easy Chicken Stir Fry	24
Chicken Pot Pie	25
Brown Gravy Beef Roast with Vegetables	26
Ham & Potatoes	27
Chilironi	28
We're Stuffed Pork Chops	29
Super Tator Tot Casserole	29
It's-So-Easy-Kabobs	30
Pot Roast Perfection	30
Best BBQ Sandwiches	31
Taco Pizza	32
Split-Second Burritos	33
Beefy Broccoli	34
Thanksgiving Pie	34
Old Fashion Chicken & Rice	35
Lasagna Rolls	36

ONE POT WONDERS

Favorite Fettuccini	36
French Toast Brunch Casserole	37
Shrimp & Spice Pasta	38
Perfect Potato Bake	38
Penne 4 Your Thoughts Pasta	38
Poor Man's Casserole	38
Cheese-A-Roni	39
Crockpot Shells	40
Curley and Moe Noodles	40
Weekend Brunch Bonanza Casserole	41
Potato Pie	42

A Sweet & Happy Ending... Delectable Desserts

Warmed Apple Sauce with Cinnamon Croutons	44
Bananarama Cream Pie	45
Crispy Peanut Butter Chocolate Pie	46
Cream Cheese Dream Bars	46
Fruit Pizza	46
Hot Fudge Mocha Shake	47
Birthday Cake Surprise	47
Cloud Dip	58
Andes™ Candies Parfaits	58

Etcetera...

A Few Things You'll Need to Know	7
One-Pot Wonders	9
Rice Is Nice	16
Moister Meat	17
Potato Peelings	21
Beef It Up	22
Quick Thickener	24
Salt S.O.S.	26
Veggie Bundles	27
Freezing Facts	28
Crock Circulation	31
Personal Shopper – List # 1	50
Personal Shopper – List # 2	53
Personal Shopper – List # 3	55

A Few Things You'll Need To Know...

Pay close attention when you see this symbol. It means that you are about to uncover a 'Mother-Knows-Best' tip which will save you countless headaches when feeding your children.

While every recipe chosen for The Rush Hour Cook™ can be prepared quickly, the recipes marked with this symbol may very well be faster than a speeding bullet. I've also used this symbol to denote recipes that save valuable time or offer make-ahead options.

At the end of this book, you'll find a section called, Your Personal Shopper. I've included pre-planned menus and grocery lists to get you through those rough weeks when you don't feel like planning - which is just about every week, for me! These are the recipes that I now use much to my family's satisfaction and success.

Serve It Up—All recipes are sized for 6 Servings, unless otherwise noted. If you have a family of 3 or 4, consider adding a few more members or better yet, make the full recipe anyway. Use the rest for lunches the following day, or freeze these extras as healthy, homemade options to those ready-made, chemical-laden convenience-meals.

High-fat, some-fat, low-fat or no-fat—Most of the recipes within this book are either low in fat or easily adaptable for low fat options. When prepared this way, the caloric and fat intakes coinciding with each meal, contain less than 30% fat.

Make Your Misto™— In most cookbooks, almost every recipe calls for cooking spray. Instead of using the aerosol cans that you can buy in the store, purchase a Misto™ or other non-aerosol pump. With these pumps, you can add a bit of olive, canola or vegetable oil and they will convert the oil to spray. This allows you to use the minimum amount of oil and avoid the nasty-chemicals found in their store-shelved counter-parts.

INTRODUCTION:
THE CREATION OF ONE-POT WONDERS

Let's be honest—the list of reasons to stay out of a kitchen are as vast as solitaire versions. Amongst the top of that list has to be the chaos that is created from cooking. When you look at the unpredictability of the American dinner hour, it's easy to see why most families only sit down together once a week—if that!

To make my point, imagine this scene . . . Parent (for the sake of the story, I'll use Mom) arrives home at 6:00 P.M. only to panic since she hasn't had a moment to contemplate dinner fare. Scrambling through the freezer, cabinets and refrigerator she disregards all thoughts of the food pyramid and instead focuses on anything consumable and non-toxic. Buried behind unfilled ice cube trays and an empty container of ice cream, Mom discovers an unknown meat in a freezer bag—presumably beef.

This will work, she thinks, quickly slapping it on a plate and hitting the auto-defrost button on her microwave. Next the water goes on the stove top for some noodles. Pulling cheese, sauce and other miscellaneous items from cabinets and drawers she recognizes enough fixings for a casserole. She grabs the casserole dish just as the beef finishes its defrost cycle. The last vacant burner goes to the frying pan as she quickly browns the beef and then piles everything into the casserole dish. Of course, during the entire preparation miscellaneous family members are drifting into the home, all of them rushing for the kitchen and a "quick snack." Protectively guarding her few precious finds for dinner, she works around the crew to navigate her casserole concoction. In 30 minutes she has dinner on the table. Not wanting it to get cold, and wanting to eat before Johnny needs a ride for play practice, she leaves the few spatters and drips to clean up later, forgetting that these things harden to the likes of epoxy-resin after 14 seconds.

Just as she rests her weary bottom in the one wobbly chair (the stable chairs had long since been claimed) Junior asks if he can be excused. Glancing at his plate, she notices that all its contents have disappeared. Junior-etta proudly announces that she has become a vegetarian since learning about animals at 4-H. Appalled that her mother could partake in the slaughter of an innocent cow, she also leaves the table.

Well, it's just the two of us, Mom thinks happily. Just then her husband puts his napkin on the table and checks his watch. He promised to take Junior-etta and friend to the hobby store for science experiment supplies. At precisely 7:04.

Her napkin finally secure in her lap, Mom takes her first bite of the semi-warm meal at the empty table while watching Junior-etta's entrée harden on its untouched plate. After all the commotion, Mom realizes sleep sounds better than food and she clears her plate from the table. After making 10 laps for the other plates and miscellaneous items on the table she confronts the small kitchen that is supposed to be a source of warm, comfort food. The sink contains stacks of dishes that would make any Tetris-player proud. The pans, which couldn't fit in the sink, still sit on the stove and the dishwasher hasn't been emptied from last night's meal.

Let's face it…who wants to cook for the average family of four then face the pile of dishes that comes after your dinner partners scarf down their meals faster than the four-year-crown-holder of the County Fair Pie Contest? Oh sure, in an ideal world someone other than the one who cooks does the cleaning. I have yet to find the appropriate vehicle to take me into that world—my guess is that you haven't either. (If by chance you do, please let me know as I am sure we could partner and make a million.)

In the meantime, I found that I could drastically reduce time spent in the kitchen and the amount of dirty dishes by unearthing recipes that could be prepared in a single pot—or a few bowls that can be easily wiped clean, plus one baking dish. I am pleased to share those with you in this volume.

As always, I feel it's important to stay focused when working on any book and I have found that setting a few rules and criteria for recipe selection truly helps the process.

The Rules for my One-Pot Wonders remain the same as my original Rush Hour Cook™ rules which you'll find below...

The Five Rules of Rush Hour Recipes:

1. All ingredients should be able to be pronounced accurately through the phonetic use of the English Language.

2. Each ingredient can be located in the market without engaging in a full scale scavenger hunt.

3. No list of ingredients shall be longer than the instructions.

4. Each recipe has to be durable enough to survive me, the Queen-of-Incapable-Cooking, and elicit a compliment at meal's end.

5. My finicky child will eat it—or some portion of it. I've learned not to be too picky on this one. I'll often break out part of the recipe and prepare it separately to her liking.

So on the nights when you can't face a pile of dishes, grab this volume and choose one of its many flavorful one-pot wonders!

In the Beginning...

Soups, Sides and Starters

Quick Recipe Index:

Pizza Dip	14
Apple Dip	14
Choose-A-Way-Breadsticks	15
Denise's Pizza Wheels	16
Aztec Salad	16
Party Pinwheels	17
Spicy Salsa	17
Join The Club Salad	18
Pretzel Dip	18
Baked Mozzarella Sticks	19
I Slaved All Day Cheddar and Herb Biscuits	20
Cheesy Potato Soup	20
Grecian Style Potatoes	21
Chicken Tortilla Soup	22

Pizza Dip

1 can(4 oz.) tomato paste
1 can (8 oz.) tomato sauce
1 tablespoon oregano
½ tablespoon minced garlic
12 chopped olives
¼ teaspoon pepper
1 cup mozzarella cheese
1 loaf French bread, cut in slices

Mix all ingredients in a saucepan except the cheese and bread and cook over low heat. Simmer for 10 minutes. Add cheese and stir constantly until cheese is melted. Serve hot with bread for dipping.

Apple Dip
Makes 8+ servings

1 (8 oz.) package cream cheese, softened
¼ cup caramel sundae sauce
½ cup sour cream
¼ cup finely chopped walnuts
6 golden delicious or red delicious apples, cored and sliced
1 tablespoon lemon juice

Mix cream cheese, caramel, sour cream and walnuts in a serving bowl. Chill for one hour to blend flavors. Slice apples and mix with lemon juice to slow browning of the apples. Serve dip with sliced apples.

Choose-A-Way Bread Sticks

Each refrigerated can of breadstick dough makes 8 breadsticks

8 Toppings to Try:

Bruchetta: chopped tomatoes, chopped fresh parsley and olive oil

Greek: chopped black or Klamatta olives, Feta cheese, and basil

Three cheese: cheddar, Parmesan and mozzarella

Ham and cheese: thinly sliced deli ham, Swiss cheese and Dijon mustard

Pizza: pepperoni, mozzarella cheese and pizza sauce

Herbed: fresh chopped oregano, basil and cilantro (or use dried)

Garlic bread: melted butter and minced garlic (1 teaspoon garlic for every 3 tablespoons butter or you will smell very nice the next day!)

Here's what to do: Preheat oven according to the package directions on the refrigerated breadsticks. Separate dough into strips. Brush dough with your choice of olive oil, melted butter, margarine, or Italian dressing. Place toppings on top of dough and twist. Brush again with oil or butter. Bake according to directions. Some fillings may fall off or ooze over the sides of the breadsticks. Don't worry...consider it edible art.

This is a great slumber party snack that is fun to both make and eat!

Denise's Pizza Wheels

Makes 8 servings

32 Ritz™ or other snack crackers
1 (6 oz.) can tomato paste
1 teaspoon oregano
1 teaspoon garlic
1 teaspoon basil
1 teaspoon pepper
1 pound ground beef, browned
1 cup cheddar cheese

Mix together tomato paste and seasonings. Preheat oven to 350 degrees. Brown ground beef. Spread tomato paste mixture on crackers and top with ground beef and a pinch of cheese. Bake in oven for 5-10 minutes or until cheese melts. Serve hot.

Aztec Salad

Makes 4 servings

1 package salad mix
1 can corn, drained
1 can black beans, drained
½ red onion chopped
½ cup tomato vinaigrette dressing

Toss all ingredients in a large salad serving bowl. Serve immediately. For a main dish meal, add ½ pound of cooked chicken.

RICE IS NICE!

You can make rice in a flash with one dish and a microwave. Simply place 1 cup of rice with 2 cups of hot water. Cook on high for about 9-10 minutes. For brown rice, use the same ratio but cook for 15-20 minutes. To add more taste, use a tablespoon or two of bouillon granules or add ½ cup of frozen peas after cooking, cover and let peas warm for 5 minutes. Cubed ham is another quick and easy addition!

Party Pinwheels

Makes 8 servings

4 large flour tortillas
1 (8 oz.) package cream cheese
½ cup sour cream
2 tablespoons Dijon mustard
4 slices ham

Mix cream cheese, sour cream and mustard in a small bowl. Spread mixture on flour tortillas. Place one slice of ham on each tortilla and two baby dill pickles down the center. Roll up and wrap individually in plastic wrap and refrigerate for one hour. Cut into 6 slices per wrap and serve.

Spicy Salsa

Makes 8 servings

15 roma tomatoes chopped
1 white onion, chopped
1 bunch of cilantro chopped
1 can green chilies

Mix all ingredients and chill for 1 hour or more. Serve with chips or with your favorite Mexican dish. If desired add corn, carrots or green peppers to this salsa. If you need a real mild salsa, (this is medium-low spice) omit the chilies all together.

MOISTER MEAT

WHEN COOKING A SOUP OR STEW, REPLACE WATER WITH WINE, TEA, BROTH OR BEER. NOT ONLY WILL EXPERIMENTING WITH THESE LIQUIDS ADD A DELICIOUS FLAVOR, THEY WILL ALSO HELP TENDERIZE MEAT.

Join The Club Salad
Makes 4 servings

1 bag salad mix
8 oz. turkey, cut into strips
8 cherry or Roma tomatoes
¼ cup crumbled bacon pieces or 4 strips
   of cooked bacon
4 pieces of toast (cut in ½ lengthwise and
   then again to form 4 rectangles)
Ranch dressing

Divide the salad mix into four bowls. Lay turkey strips across the mix. Garnish each salad with two tomatoes (can be halved if desired) and divide the bacon pieces among the salad. Garnish each salad with the four toast points by sticking the toast points evenly around the bowl. Serve with ranch dressing on the side.

Pretzel Dip
Makes 8 servings

¼ cup sugar
2 tablespoons Dijon mustard
½ teaspoon dry mustard
2 teaspoons vegetable oil
1 cup mayonnaise
½ tablespoon garlic powder

Mix all ingredients and refrigerate for at least one hour. Serve with pretzel sticks or soft pretzels (available in the frozen food section).

Baked Mozzarella Sticks

Makes 4 servings

2 eggs
1 tablespoon water
1 cup Italian dry bread crumbs
1 teaspoon garlic powder
¼ teaspoon pepper
½ cup corn flakes crushed
½ cup flour
12 sticks string cheese
1 cup prepared spaghetti sauce

Beat eggs and water in a small bowl to form an egg wash. In a separate bowl, mix breadcrumbs, garlic powder, pepper and corn flakes. Place flour in a separate bowl. Dip each stick of cheese into flour, then egg wash, and then bread crumb mixture until fully coated (may have to repeat). Put on ungreased baking sheet and cover and freeze for one hour. Preheat oven to 400 degrees and bake for 7-9 minutes or until golden brown and crispy. To serve, dip in heated spaghetti sauce.

I Slaved All Day Cheddar and Herb Biscuits

Makes 8 servings

1 tube of refrigerated biscuits
3 tablespoons butter or margarine
1 tablespoon garlic powder, pepper and
   dill (or any other seasoning)
1 cup shredded cheddar cheese

Preheat oven to 375 or as directed on the package. Melt butter and mix with seasonings. Brush butter mixture over the biscuits   Top biscuits with cheddar cheese. Bake for 12 minutes or as directed on the package. You can serve these biscuits without butter, because they are sooooo tasty!

Cheesy Potato Soup

Makes 4 servings

1 box augratin
   potatoes
1 can corn, drained
1 can beer, optional
3 cups water
1 cup milk
2 cups shredded
   cheddar cheese

In pot combine all ingredients, except for shredded cheese. Stir well. Bring to a boil, reduce heat and simmer for 20 minutes. Add shredded cheese. Stir constantly until cheese is well blended. Serve. For a main dish, add sliced cooked bratwurst or any type of sausage.

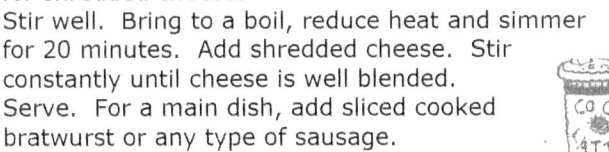

When preparing for kids, either omit the beer or separate an alcohol free portion for them.

Grecian Style Potatoes

Makes 4 servings

6 slices cooked crumbled bacon
3 potatoes sliced very thinly
1 small onion thinly sliced
1 (4 oz.) package crumbled Feta cheese
1 tablespoon oregano
1 teaspoon basil
1 cup crushed tomatoes

Cook onions till tender. Add potatoes, bacon, oregano and basil. Cook until potatoes are tender about 15 minutes over medium low heat. Stir in tomatoes and heat through. Remove from heat and toss potato mixture with Feta cheese.

On a child's portion, you may want to opt for a cheese other than Feta.

POTATO PEELINGS...

While I'm not one of those who subscribes to a bunch of kitchen tools and gadgets, I have fallen in love with one handy contraption. Sold by the Pampered Chef, this potato/apple peeler mounts on your counter much like a vice. You place the potato on one end and then use the peeler to move in circular motions to remove the peel. Not only is this quick and easy but the potato peelings can be frozen and cooked as "curly fries" for a quick, kid-friendly snack.

Chicken Tortilla Soup

1 teaspoon olive oil
1 medium chopped onion
2 garlic cloves, minced
2 chicken breasts cooked and chopped (or use Louis rich™ chicken pieces)
1 cup corn
1 tablespoon hot sauce (optional)
1 teaspoon ground cumin
1 teaspoon Worcestershire sauce
1 teaspoon chili powder
2 cans chicken broth
1 (14.5 oz.) diced Mexican tomatoes, undrained
1 can tomato soup
20 tortilla chips

Heat oil in Dutch oven over medium-high heat. Add onion and garlic and sauté for 2-3 minutes. Stir in chicken, corn, hot sauce (if desired), cumin, Worcestershire sauce, chili powder, chicken broth, tomatoes and tomato soup. Simmer for 45 minutes to one hour to meld the flavors. Break tortilla chips in small bite size pieces. Top each bowl of soup with a generous amount of chips.

*ALTHOUGH THIS RECIPE HAS A FEW MORE INGREDIENTS THAN MY NORMAL RECIPES, IT'S WELL WORTH IT WHEN YOU TASTE IT! MAKE EXTRA AND FREEZE FOR 2-3 MONTHS.

BEEF IT UP

TO THICKEN STEWS AND CASSEROLES TRY ADDING A FEW TABLESPOONS OF BREADCRUMBS.

A Merry Middle...
Main Meals in Minutes

Quick Recipe Index:

WAY Easy Chicken Stir Fry	24
Chicken Pot Pie	25
Brown Gravy Beef Roast with Vegetables	26
Ham & Potatoes	27
Chilironi	28
We're Stuffed Pork Chops	29
Super Tator Tot Casserole	29
It's-So-Easy-Kabobs	30
Pot Roast Perfection	30
Best BBQ Sandwiches	31
Taco Pizza	32
Split-Second Burritos	33
Beefy Broccoli	34
Thanksgiving Pie	34
Old Fashion Chicken & Rice	35
Lasagna Rolls	36
Favorite Fettuccini	36
French Toast Brunch Casserole	37
Shrimp & Spice Pasta	38
Perfect Potato Bake	38
Penne 4 Your Thoughts Pasta	38
Poor Man's Casserole	38
Cheese-A-Roni	39
Crockpot Shells	40
Curley and Moe Noodles	40
Weekend Brunch Bonanza Casserole	41
Potato Pie	42

ONE POT WONDERS

WAY Easy Chicken Stir Fry

Makes 4 servings

1 tablespoon soy sauce
1 tablespoon ketchup
2 teaspoons ground ginger, or grate some fresh (yeah, like that will happen!)
2 cloves garlic, pressed
3 skinless, boneless chicken breasts, sliced thin
1 tablespoon oil
1 tablespoon sesame oil
6 green onions, sliced thick
1 small green pepper, sliced thin
1 small red pepper, sliced thin
4 cups cooked rice (I use brown)

Mix soy sauce, ketchup, ginger and garlic in re-sealable heavy-duty plastic bag. Add chicken; seal bag and turn to coat with marinade. Let stand 15 minutes while you cut up the veggies. Heat 1 tablespoon of the oil in 10-inch skillet or wok over medium-high heat. Add green onions and bell peppers; stir-frying until crisp-tender. Remove from skillet. Heat the remaining 1 tablespoon sesame oil in skillet and add the chicken, quickly stir-frying about 5 minutes or less, until chicken is cooked. Stir in bell pepper mixture. Serve on brown rice.

Excerpted from: The Frantic Family Cookbook(Mostl) Healthy Meals in Minutes by Leanne Ely, C.N.C. (ISBN 1-891400-11-8, www.championpress.com)

Quick Thickener

Thicken soups, casseroles and sauces with a mixture of cornstarch and water. Mix until a smooth paste if formed and then add to the liquid.

Chicken Pot Pie

1 can cream of chicken soup
1 can cream of potato soup
1 can skim milk
3-4 chicken breasts, cooked, skinned and de-boned
2 cups frozen peas and carrots, cooked and drained
3-4 potatoes, peeled and cubed, cooked and drained
1 small to medium onion, diced finely
2 packages refrigerated biscuits
1 teaspoon salt
½ teaspoon pepper
½ teaspoon celery flakes
½ teaspoon parsley flakes

In a 9 x 13 casserole-baking dish, combine soups with milk and seasoning. Break up chicken into bite-sized pieces and stir into soups. Add cooked peas and carrots, potatoes and the fresh onion. Bake at 400 degrees for 20 minutes. Remove casserole dish from oven and place prepared biscuits on top of the chicken and vegetable mixture, covering the entire dish. Return dish to oven, reduce heat to 350 degrees and bake until the biscuits are golden brown—about 20-25 minutes.

Brown Gravy Beef Roast With Vegetables

1 (3-5 pound) beef, roast, trimmed of visible fat
2 packets brown gravy mix
2 cups water
6-9 medium potatoes, peeled and halved
4-6 large carrots, cut in pieces
1 onion, sliced
1 cup fresh sliced mushrooms, optional
1 teaspoon salt
½ teaspoon black pepper

Set meat in crockpot and sprinkle with salt. Arrange vegetables around meat. In saucepan, prepare gravy mixes with water according to package directions. Pour over meat and vegetables. Sprinkle salt and pepper over vegetables. Cover with lid and cook on high for 7-9 hours.

Excerpted from: Crazy About Crockpots, 101 Easy and Inexpensive Recipes for Less than .75 a Serving by Penny E Stone(ISBN 1-891400-12-6, www.championpress.com)

Salt S.O.S.

NEXT TIME YOU FIND YOURSELF WITH A TOO-SALTY STEW-DON'T DESPAIR! GRAB A POTATO, CUT IT INTO 1-INCH CHUNKS AND TOSS IT IN THE POT. ONCE THE POTATO IS SOFT, REMOVE IT FROM THE STEW. THIS WILL HELP DRAW OUT EXCESS SALT.

Ham & Potatoes

Makes 8+ servings

10 medium potatoes, peeled and sliced
1 teaspoon salt
½ teaspoon pepper
1 onion, chopped
2 lbs. baked ham, cut in thin strips or diced in small squares
1 pkg. Instant dry onion soup mix
1 can cream of mushroom soup
1 soup can water
2 cups shredded cheddar cheese
1 cup American processed cheese spread

Combine all ingredients in crockpot and mix well. Cover with lid and cook on low for 6 hours or until potatoes are tender.

Excerpted from: Crazy about Crockpots! 101 Recipes for Entertaining at Less than .75 a serving by Penny E Stone (ISBN 1-891400-53-3, www.championpress.com)

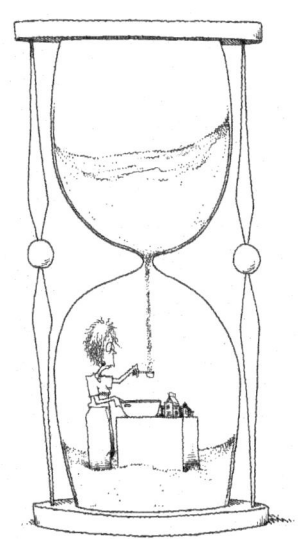

Veggie Bundles

Slice and dice a mixture of potatoes and vegetables, add a dab of butter and fold into a tightly-sealed aluminum foil packet. Place packets in with roasts during the last hour of cooking. Experiment with adding different herbs, salt and pepper for seasoning.

Chilironi

Makes 4 servings

1 pound ground beef
1 onion chopped
1 (14.5 oz.) can of Mexican stewed tomatoes
1 cup V-8™
1 (8 oz.) can of tomato sauce
2 teaspoons chili powder
½ teaspoon pepper
1 can corn, drained
1 (8 oz.) package elbow macaroni
1 cup shredded cheddar cheese
hot sauce, if desired (or just serve on the side)

Brown ground beef in skillet. While browning beef, cook pasta according to directions. Add onion to ground beef and sauté for 5 minutes. Add tomatoes, V-8™ and tomato sauce and bring to a slight boil. Reduce heat and add seasoning. Simmer for 15-20 minutes. Add macaroni and stir until heated through. Serve in a big bowl with ¼ cup cheese. Great with a side salad! If making a kid friendly meal, you might want to hold the onions and serve them on the side for the adults!

Freezing Facts

Most soups and stews can easily be frozen for quick preparation later. When freezing make sure to leave an inch of space near the top of the container for any liquid that expands as it freezes. Also, use a black Sharpie® permanent marker to label containers and the date frozen. This will help avoid "mystery dinner." Another bright freezing idea is to prepare extra servings that can intentionally be saved for another day (I call these right-overs instead of left-overs.) For best reheating results, undercook these dishes slightly before freezing

We're Stuffed Pork Chops
Makes 4 servings

4 butterfly pork chops
1 pkg. prepared Stove Top™ stuffing
1 package frozen mixed veggies
¼ cup water
1 can cream of mushroom soup

Heat oven to 375 degrees. Place frozen veggies in bottom of 13 x 9 casserole dish. Place prepared stuffing on top of veggies. Place butterfly chops on top of stuffing. Mix canned soup with ¼ cup water and pour over chop, stuffing and veggie mixture. Bake for 35-45 minutes until chops are done.

When there is only five ingredients, you know it has to e easy!

Souper Tator Tot Casserole
1 pound ground beef, browned
1 package frozen tator tots
1 can French green beans, drained
1 can cream of mushroom soup
1 can sliced mushrooms, drained
½ cup milk
1 teaspoon salt
1 tablespoon pepper

Layer ground beef, tots and beans in 9 x 13 casserole dish. Mix soup, mushrooms, milk, salt and pepper in separate dish and pour over casserole. Cover and bake for 35 minutes. Uncover and bake for 10 minutes more or until golden brown. Serve with biscuits or warm rolls.

It's-So-Easy-Kabobs

Makes 4 servings

1 lb. meat (chicken or beef cut into one inch pieces or use peeled shrimp)
8 whole mushrooms, washed
1 green pepper, sliced in 1 inch pieces
8 cherry tomatoes
1 zucchini, sliced in 1 inch pieces
1 onion, sliced in large chunks
½ cup teriyaki sauce

Marinate meat in teriyaki sauce for 1 hour. Skewer as follows: mushroom, green pepper, meat, onion, tomato, meat, zucchini, and repeat. Brush entire skewer with teriyaki sauce. Grill for 10 minutes on each side. Serve with rice or other starch.

Pot Roast Perfection

3 pound beef roast
1 pound onions, sliced
1 12 oz. bottle of beer
1 package oxtail soup mix

In a large pan mix ⅛ cup water with onions and stir for five minutes. Transfer onions to crock pot. Add beer, soup mix and 1 cup water to crock pot and stir well. Place meat in mixture and cook on low setting for 6-8 hours. Let stand 10 minutes before serving.
Fast... easy... perfect!

If making for children as well, try substituting beef broth for the beer.

Best BBQ Sandwiches

Makes 8 servings

6 tablespoons brown sugar
1 teaspoon black pepper
2 pounds flank steak
1 cup onion, chopped
1 cup tomato sauce
1 cup tomato paste
4 tablespoon Worcestershire sauces
4 tablespoons cider vinegar
1 tablespoon chili powder
1 tablespoon garlic powder
1 teaspoon dry mustard
1 teaspoon ground cumin
½ teaspoon salt
sandwich rolls, 1 per person

Combine brown sugar and pepper, then rub over steaks. Combine all remaining ingredients (except the sandwich rolls of course) in a crock pot. Cook on low for 7 hours. Shred steak with forks. Stir so shredded steak is mixed well. Serve on sandwich rolls.

Crock Circulation
To promote even cooking in crockpot, help air circulate by placing the meat on top of the vegetables.

Taco Pizza

Makes 8 servings

Taco leftovers? Here's the solution!

1 loaf Rhodes™ bread dough, thawed
1 cup taco sauce
Left over taco meat and toppings
crushed tortilla chips or hard shelled tacos

Preheat oven to 375 degrees. Grease cookie sheet and roll out bread dough to fit sheet. Cover dough with the taco sauce or you can substitute salsa. Add taco meat, black olives, onions, tomatoes, lettuce and cheese. Bake for 20-25 minutes or until bubbly and crust is golden brown. Serve with crushed tortilla chips/shells and sour cream on the side. For those adventurous types, add jalapeno peppers and hot sauce!

Make A Tantalizing Turkey

When cooking a turkey, try laying down a "bed" of celery stalks first. The stalks will help air circulate and keep the turkey moist while also adding great flavor. Another great tip for keeping your turkey moist is to roast it breast-side down for the first hour and then turn it over for the remainder of the cooking time.

Split Second Burritos

1 pound ground beef
1 onion, chopped
2 tablespoons chili powder
1 can refried beans
6 large flour tortillas
1 (8 oz.) can enchilada sauce
2 cups shredded cheddar cheese
salsa
sour cream
black olives

Brown ground beef and onion in skillet. Mix in chili powder. Microwave tortillas for 30 seconds to soften. Divide beans and meat on to the 6 tortillas. Fold tortillas over the meat/bean mixture and place in microwave dish, seam side down. Top with enchilada sauce and cheese. Microwave 2-4 minutes (depending on wattage of oven) until cheese is melted and burritos are heated through. Top according to taste with salsa, sour cream and black olives.

A quick, easy and split-second dish.

Beefy Broccoli
Makes 4 servings

1 pound lean boneless beef steak (top round, flank or sirloin)
1 pound broccoli florets
2 tablespoons soy sauce
1 tablespoon garlic, minced
1 (10.5 oz.) can beef gravy

Cut beef with the grain into 1½ inch wide strips, then cut each strip into ¼ inch diagonal slices. Mix beef strips with soy sauce and garlic in a bowl. Set aside to marinate. Steam broccoli in microwave steamer for 4 minutes until crisp tender. (If you don't have a steamer, use a microwave safe bowl with ¼ cup water and cover with plastic wrap). Stir fry beef over medium high heat in skillet until browned on all sides (2-3 minutes each side). Add broccoli and beef gravy and cook until heated through. Serve hot with steamed rice.

Thanksgiving Pie
3 cups stuffing
1½ cups turkey, cubed or shredded
1 (10.5) ounce can cream of mushroom soup
½ cup chopped celery
½ cup chopped onion
1 teaspoon pepper

Combine all ingredients in a 1 quart casserole dish adding a bit or broth or water if mixture is dry. Bake in a 350 degree oven for 30-40 minutes or until heated through.

Old-Fashioned Chicken and Rice

2½ cups canned fat-free chicken broth
1½ pounds boneless skinless chicken breasts, cut into 1-inch pieces
1½ cups long-grain rice, uncooked
1 cup onion, chopped
¼ cup fresh parsley, minced
6 garlic cloves, minced
1 small red bell pepper, sliced into thin strips
1 (6 oz.) jar sliced mushrooms, undrained
1 teaspoon poultry seasonings

Cut up chicken into 1-inch pieces. Chop onions. Mince cloves and parsley. Slice red bell pepper into long thin strips. In large saucepan or Dutch oven, bring broth to a boil. Add remaining ingredients. Mix well and return to boil. Reduce heat to medium; cover tightly and cook 20 minutes or until chicken is no longer pink and rice is tender. Serve.

Excerpted from: Frozen Assets Lite and Easy by Deborah Taylor-Hough.(ISBN 1-89140-019-3, www.championpress.com)

ONE POT WONDERS

Lasagna Rolls

1 pound ground turkey or beef
1 (16 oz.) container cottage cheese
2 cups mozzarella cheese
1 tablespoon garlic
1 tablespoon oregano
1 (24 oz.) jar of prepared spaghetti sauce
1 package lasagna noodles

Preheat oven to 350 degrees. Prepare noodles according to package directions, set aside. Mix cottage cheese and 1 cup mozzarella cheese, set aside. Brown ground beef or turkey with garlic and oregano. Place ⅛ cup ground meat mixture on noodles and spread cheese mixture over meat. Roll and place in 9 x 13 inch baking pan. Repeat with rest of the noodles. Pour spaghetti sauce over noodles in pan and sprinkle remaining cheese over rolls. Bake for 35-45 minutes covered or until sauce is bubbly and cheese is melted.

Consider freezing in individual size servings for a quick and easy re-heated option.

Favorite Fettuccini

1 cup evaporated skim milk
½ cup Parmesan cheese, grated
1 pound fettuccini, cooked
¼ teaspoon white pepper

Heat milk over medium heat being careful not to boil. Add cheese until sauce thickens. Remove from heat and toss with fettuccini. Season to taste.

French Toast Brunch Casserole

12 slices cinnamon raisin bread
4 tablespoons butter or margarine, melted
4 eggs, beaten
2 cups milk
2 tablespoons maple syrup
2 teaspoons vanilla
1 teaspoon nutmeg
syrup for serving
powdered sugar

Preheat oven to 350 degrees. Lightly grease 9 x 13 baking pan. Place the bread in the dish in two layers. Mix butter, eggs, milk, syrup, vanilla and nutmeg together well. Pour egg mixture over bread to coat thoroughly. Make sure all bread is saturated with the mixture. Bake uncovered for 45 minutes uncovered. Cut into squares and serve with warm syrup and powdered sugar. Serve with fresh fruit and coffee for a full brunch meal.

Simple & Speedy Pasta Bake

1 tablespoon olive oil
3 cloves garlic, minced
1 (28-ounce) can tomatoes, crushed
1 pound pasta
2 cups mozzarella or cheddar cheese

Cook garlic in oil over medium heat in a large, ovenproof dish. Add tomatoes. Salt and pepper to taste. Cook for five minutes and then add the pasta and 1 cup grated cheese. Cover with the other cup of cheese. Baked in 350 degree oven for 20 minutes or until heated through and cheese is bubbly.

Perfect Potato Bake

Makes 8 servings

1 (16 oz.) pkg. frozen hashbrown potatoes
1 green pepper chopped
2 cups frozen green peas
1 medium onion, chopped
2 cups cheddar cheese
1 tablespoon pepper
½ tablespoon salt

Sauté green pepper and onion in 1 tablespoon oil for five minutes. Add potatoes and cook over medium heat, stirring often, until hashbrowns are lightly browned. Add peas, salt and pepper. Transfer to 9 x 13 baking dish and cover with cheddar cheese. Bake in 350 degree oven for 20-30 minutes.

Poor Man's Casserole

2 cups ground round, browned
1 lb. frozen vegetables
3 cups mashed potatoes
1 cup yellow cheese, grated
seasonings to taste

Mix meat with vegetables and place in 9 x 13-inch casserole dish. Add spices. Spread mashed potatoes over top of meat and vegetable mixture. Sprinkle grated cheese over top of potatoes. Bake uncovered in 350 degree oven for 20-30 minutes or until heated through.

Penne 4 Your Thoughts Pasta

1 (12 oz.) package penne pasta
1 pound ground beef
1 (24 oz.) jar of prepared spaghetti sauce
1 (8 oz.) package sliced mushrooms, sautéed
1 cup shredded mozzarella cheese

Preheat oven to 350 degrees. Prepare pasta according to package directions and drain. Cook meat in skillet over medium high heat and drain fat. Stir in prepared spaghetti sauce and sautéed mushrooms   Cook for 7-8 minutes. Mix with pasta and transfer to a 13x9 inch baking dish. Sprinkle cheese over dish and cover. Bake for 20 minutes.

Cheese-A-Roni

Makes 4 servings

1 (12 oz.) package elbow macaroni
2 cups shredded cheese
1 cup milk
⅔ cup cottage cheese
½ teaspoon pepper
½ teaspoon salt

Preheat oven to 350 degrees.
Combine all ingredients in a baking dish and bake for 30 minutes. Add any favorite vegetable to this dish.

Curly and Moe Noodles
Makes 4 servings

1 tablespoon vegetable oil
1 pound chicken breast strips
2 packages chicken flavored Ramen™ noodles
1½ cup water
1 cup broccoli flowerets
1 tablespoon soy sauce
½ tablespoon garlic

Heat oil in skillet over medium high heat. Add chicken and stir fry about 5-8 minutes until chicken is cooked all the way through. Break apart noodles. Stir noodles, seasonings from flavor packet, water, broccoli, soy sauce and garlic in the skillet. Bring to a boil and boil for 3-4 minutes (stirring often) until noodles are done.

Crockpot Shells
1 pound ground turkey
2 cloves garlic, minced
2 cups mozzarella cheese
½ cup bread crumbs
1 egg, beaten
18 jumbo pasta shells, cooked and drained
2 (15.5 oz.) jars prepared spaghetti sauce
½ cup Parmesan cheese, grated

Brown beef and garlic and then drain. Add mozzarella cheese, bread crumbs and egg. Stuff shells with mixture. Pour first jar of sauce into bottom of crockpot and then arrange shells. Cover with the 2nd jar of sauce. Top with Parmesan. Cook for 6 to 7 hours on low setting.

Weekend Brunch Bonanza (casserole)

Makes 8 servings

THIS IS BEST WHEN MADE THE NIGHT BEFORE AND REFRIGERATED OVERNIGHT.

1 lb. pork sausage links cut into small pieces cooked
4 cups cubed day-old French or white bread
2 cups (16 oz.) shredded cheddar cheese
2 cans evaporated milk (not condensed)
12 eggs, lightly beaten
1 teaspoon season salt
1 tablespoon pepper
1 medium onion, optional
1 green pepper, chopped, optional

Preheat oven to 325 degrees. Grease baking dish. Place bread cubes in dish. Sprinkle with 1 cup of the cheese. Combine milk, eggs, season salt, pepper, onion and green pepper and pour over bread cubes. Top with cooked sausage and remaining 1 cup of cheese. Bake for 1 hour, uncovered. Let cool for 10 minutes before serving. Can assemble the night before and bake the next day. Increase baking time if dish is put cold into the oven.

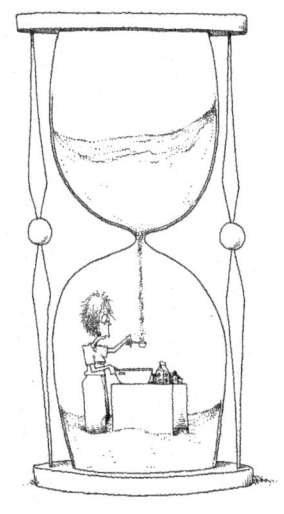

Potato Pie

1 cup Miracle Whip
¼ cup flour
1 teaspoon salt
½ teaspoon pepper
1¼ cup milk
½ teaspoon dried basil
2 cups chicken, chopped
2 cups potatoes, mashed
1 (10 oz.) package frozen vegetables, thawed
1½ cups cheddar cheese, divided

Mix all ingredients except for potatoes over medium-high heat in a 2-quart casserole dish. Cook for 5 minutes. Top with potato mixture. Broil until golden then top with ½ cup cheddar cheese and broil until the cheese is slightly melted.

Adults:
Consider adding 8 oz. mushrooms, sliced
1/3 cup onion, diced

A Sweet & Happy Ending...
Delectable Desserts

Quick Recipe Index:

Warmed Apple Sauce with Cinnamon Croutons	44
Bananarama Cream Pie	45
Crispy Peanut Butter Chocolate Pie	46
Cream Cheese Dream Bars	46
Fruit Pizza	46
Hot Fudge Mocha Shake	47
Birthday Cake Surprise	47
Cloud Dip	48
Andes™ Candies Parfaits	48

Warmed Apple Sauce with Cinnamon Croutons

3 tablespoons sugar
¾ teaspoon ground cinnamon
1 French baguette, sliced into 12 slices
½ cup apple butter
3 cups warmed chunky apple sauce

Combine sugar and cinnamon in shallow dish; stir well, and set aside. Brush both sides of bread slices with apple butter and fry till golden, turning once. Drain on paper towels and top with cinnamon sugar mixture. Warm applesauce and serve with croutons.

Excerpted from: Fry it...You'll Like it! By Olivia Friedman.(ISBN 1-891400-55-1, www.championpress.com)

Bananarama Cream Pie

Makes 8 servings

1 (6 oz.) graham cracker crust
1 (1.4 oz.) pkg. vanilla instant pudding
1⅓ cups milk
1 (8 oz.) tub of whipped topping
2 medium bananas, sliced

Make pudding using 1⅓ cup cold milk. Put ½ cup of the whipped topping on the bottom of the crust. Place one sliced banana over the whipped topping. Top with pudding and place the other sliced banana over the pudding. Top with additional whipped topping. Chill for 1 hour minimum or until set. This can be made the night before.

Crispy Peanut Butter Chocolate Pie

¼ cup creamy peanut butter
1 tablespoon butter or margarine
1½ cups Rice Krispie® cereal
1 pkg. chocolate fudge instant pudding
1⅓ cup milk
1 (8 oz.) tub of whipped topping
½ cup of Reeses Pieces®

Put butter and peanut butter in microwave safe bowl. Heat until melted and pour over cereal. Stir to coat. Pour cereal mixture into bottom of greased pie pan and press down to form crust. Use wax paper or a wooden spoon to make this easier to spread). Make pudding according to pie filling directions on package. Fold one cup of the whipped topping into the pudding. Pour into the crust. Top with the remaining whipped topping. Garnish with Reeses Pieces®. Chill for 2 hours before serving.

Cream Cheese Dream Bars

Makes 8 servings

2 (8 oz.) packages refrigerated crescent rolls, seperated
2 (8 oz.) packages cream cheese
1 cup plus ½ cup sugar divided
1 egg, separated
1 teaspoon vanilla
½ cup sugar
½ chopped pecans or walnuts
1 teaspoon cinnamon

Preheat oven to 350 degrees. Place 1 pkg. separated crescent rolls in the bottom of a 9 x 13 inch pan. Stretch the dough to fit the bottom. Poke a few holes in the dough with a fork. Mix cream cheese, sugar, egg yoke and vanilla until smooth. Spread over crust. Separate second package of rolls and arrange over the top. Combine sugar, nuts, and cinnamon in a small bowl, set aside. In another bowl beat egg white until frothy. Brush top crust with egg white. Sprinkle nut topping over the crust. Bake for 30 minutes or until golden brown.

Fruit Pizza

Makes 8 servings

1 tube refrigerated sugar cookie dough
1 container strawberry cream cheese fruit dip
2 cups assorted fresh fruit (grapes, kiwi, strawberries, raspberries, blueberries, cherries)

Roll out cookie dough to fit pizza pan. Bake at 375 degrees for 12-15 minutes until golden brown. Cool. Spread fruit dip on top of baked dough and top with sliced fresh fruit of your choice. For a quicker, cheaper version, you can use well drained fruit cocktail, but fresh fruit is the best. Slice into serving pieces, either squares or triangles.

Hot Fudge Mocha Shake

Makes 4 servings

4 cups coffee ice cream
½ cup hot fudge topping
1 cup milk

Put all items in a blender and mix for 1 minute or until of desired consistency. I use the puree setting on my blender. If you are not a coffee lover, use vanilla ice cream. If you are a coffee lover, add 1 tablespoon ground coffee beans to the mix before blending. Serve with a spoon and enjoy!

Birthday Cake Surprise

Makes 12 servings

1 pkg. cake mix, prepared according to
 directions but not baked
aluminum Foil
12 Hershey Kisses™
1 quart ice cream
chocolate, strawberry or butterscotch
 topping

Mix cake mix as directed on box. Line a cupcake pan with paper liners. Pour cake mix in each cup filling only ½ of cup. Make 12 foil balls about 1 inch in diameter, and place one in middle of each cupcake. Make sure that each foil ball is sticking out of the cake mix. Bake as directed on package. Allow the cup cakes to cool for about 30 minutes before removing the foil ball. Remove carefully and place a Hershey kiss™ candy in the hole. Serve filled with ice cream and choice of toppings.

Cloud Dip

Makes 8 servings

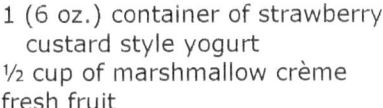

1 (8 oz.) package of cream cheese, softened
1 (6 oz.) container of strawberry custard style yogurt
½ cup of marshmallow crème
fresh fruit

Mix softened cream cheese, yogurt, and marshmallow crème in a serving bowl. Chill for one hour. Serve with fresh fruit.

Andes™ Candies Parfaits

Makes 4 servings

1 package Andes™ candies
1 (8 oz.) package whipped topping
1 package instant chocolate pudding
1¾ cup milk

Put 18 of the Andes™ candies in a plastic bag, crush with a rolling pin and set aside. Make pudding by adding the milk and refrigerate. Mix crushed Andes™ candies with ½ of the whipped topping. Divide pudding in half. Place ¼ of the pudding into four parfait dishes. Top each parfait with ¼ of the whipped topping/candy mixture. Top with remaining pudding and then the remaining whipped topping. Garnish the top of each parfait with remaining candies. Serve well-chilled.

Your Personal Shopper

As the former Queen of Non-Cooking Excuses, one of those I used most often was that I just didn't have enough time to get organized, plan and get everything from the store. To avoid the same excuse-ridden fate in your future, I am including Your Personal Shopper right in this cookbook. You have three different five-day menus to choose from. You'll find a grocery list for each of those meal plans as well.

Your Personal Shopping List # 1

Your Five-Day Menu :
1. Way Easy Chicken Stir Fry (24) followed by a dessert Andes Candies Parfaits(50)
2. Brown Gravy Beef Roast with Vegetables (26) followed by Birthday Cake Surprise (49)
3. Chilironi (28) serve with Aztec Salad (16)
4. Beefy Broccoli (34) serve with Join the Club Salad (18)
5. Perfect potato Bake (38) serve with Chicken Tortilla Soup (22)

MEATS
- ☐ 5 skinless boneless chicken breasts
- ☐ 3-5 lb. beef roast
- ☐ 1 lb. ground beef
- ☐ 1 lb. lean boneless beef steak
- ☐ 8 oz. turkey
- ☐ 1 pkg. bacon

PRODUCE
- ☐ 6 green onions
- ☐ 2 green peppers
- ☐ 1 red pepper
- ☐ 9 potatoes
- ☐ 6 carrots
- ☐ 8 cherry or Roma tomatoes
- ☐ 1 cup mushrooms
- ☐ 3 onions
- ☐ 2 pkg. salad mix
- ☐ 1 red onion
- ☐ 1 lb. broccoli florets

DRY AND CANNED GOODS
- ☐ 4 cups rice
- ☐ 1 pkg. instant chocolate pudding
- ☐ 2 packets brown gravy mix

- ☐ 1 pkg. cake mix
- ☐ 2 cans 14½ oz. Mexican stewed tomatoes
- ☐ 1 cup V-8™
- ☐ 8 oz. can tomato sauce
- ☐ 3 cans corn
- ☐ 8 oz. pkg. elbow macaroni
- ☐ 1 can black beans
- ☐ 1 can beef gravy
- ☐ 2 cans chicken broth
- ☐ 1 can tomato soup

Dairy
- ☐ 8 oz. whipped topping
- ☐ 1¾ cup milk
- ☐ 1 qt. ice cream
- ☐ 3 cups cheddar cheese

Frozen
- ☐ 16 oz. pkg. hash brown potatoes

Spice List
- ☐ soy sauce
- ☐ ketchup
- ☐ ground ginger
- ☐ 1 tbsp. oil
- ☐ 1 tbsp. sesame oil
- ☐ olive oil
- ☐ salt and pepper
- ☐ 2 tsp. chili powder
- ☐ garlic
- ☐ ground cumin
- ☐ Worcestershire sauce

Other Stuff
- ☐ 1 pkg. Andes™ candies
- ☐ aluminum foil
- ☐ 12 Hershey Kisses™
- ☐ Chocolate, strawberry or butterscotch topping
- ☐ ½ cup tomato vinaigrette dressing
- ☐ 4 pieces toast
- ☐ ranch dressing

- ☐ hot sauce (optional)
- ☐ 20 tortilla chips

Add Your Own Items:

Your Personal Shopping List # 2

Your Five-Day Menu:
1. Ham and Potatoes (27) serve with I Slaved All Day Cheddar and Herb Biscuits (20)
2. Pot Roast Perfection (30) serve with Grecian Style Potatoes (21)
3. Taco Pizza (32) and Apple Dip (14) for dessert
4. Old Fashioned Chicken and Rice (35) and a Hot Fudge Mocha Shake (48)
5. Curly and Moe Noodles (40) serve with Cheesy Potato Soup (20)

Meats
- ☐ 2 lbs. baked ham
- ☐ 3 lbs. beef roast
- ☐ bacon
- ☐ 1 lb. ground beef
- ☐ 2½ lbs. boneless skinless chicken breasts

Produce
- ☐ 4 onions
- ☐ 13 potatoes
- ☐ 6 golden delicious or red delicious apples
- ☐ ¼ cup fresh parsley
- ☐ 1 red pepper
- ☐ handful of mushrooms
- ☐ 1 cup broccoli flowerets
- ☐ 6 cloves garlic

Dry and Canned Goods
- ☐ 1 pkg. instant dry onion soup mix
- ☐ 1 can cream of mushroom soup
- ☐ 1 pkg. oxtail soup mix
- ☐ 1 cup crushed tomatoes
- ☐ 1 cup taco sauce
- ☐ 2½ cups canned fat-free chicken broth
- ☐ 1½ cup long grain rice

- ☐ 2 pkg. chicken flavored ramen noodles
- ☐ 1 box au gratin potatoes
- ☐ 1 can corn

Dairy
- ☐ 5 cups shredded cheddar cheese
- ☐ 1 cup American processed cheese spread
- ☐ 3 tbs. butter or margarine
- ☐ 4 oz. Feta cheese
- ☐ 8 oz. cream cheese
- ☐ ½ cup sour cream
- ☐ 1 qt. milk

Frozen
- ☐ 1 loaf of Rhodes bread dough
- ☐ 1 qt Mocha ice cream

Spice List
- ☐ salt and pepper
- ☐ garlic powder
- ☐ dill seasoning
- ☐ oregano
- ☐ basil
- ☐ poultry seasonings

Other Stuff
- ☐ 1 tube of refrigerated biscuits
- ☐ 2 (12oz.) bottle of beer
- ☐ bag of tortilla chips
- ☐ caramel sundae sauce
- ☐ small bag of walnuts
- ☐ lemon juice
- ☐ Hot Fudge topping
- ☐ vegetable oil
- ☐ soy sauce

Add Your Own Items:

Your Personal Shopping List # 3

Your Five-Day Menu:
1. We're Stuffed Pork Chops (29) served with Grecian Style Potatoes (21)
2. Souper Tator Tot Casserole (29)
3. Best BBQ Sandwiches (31) served with Fruit Pizza (48)
4. Chicken Pot Pie (25) followed by Bananarana Cream pie (45)
5. Spit Second Burritos (33) served with Spicy Salsa (17)

Meats
- ☐ 4 butterfly pork chops
- ☐ 1 lb. bacon
- ☐ 2 lb. ground beef
- ☐ 2 lb. flank steak
- ☐ 4 chicken breasts

Produce
- ☐ 5 lb. bag potatoes
- ☐ 5 onions
- ☐ 2 cups assorted fresh fruit
- ☐ grapes, kiwi, strawberry, raspberries, blueberries, cherries
- ☐ 2 medium bananas
- ☐ 15 Roma tomatoes
- ☐ 1 bunch cilantro

Dry and Canned Goods
- ☐ 1 pkg. stove top stuffing
- ☐ 2 cans cream of mushroom soup
- ☐ 1 can crushed tomatoes
- ☐ 1 can French green beans
- ☐ 1 can sliced mushrooms
- ☐ 1 cup tomato sauce
- ☐ 1 cup tomato paste
- ☐ 1 can cream of chicken soup

- ☐ 1 can cream of potato soup
- ☐ 1 can skim milk
- ☐ 1 pkg. vanilla instant pudding
- ☐ 1 can refried beans
- ☐ 1 can green chilies
- ☐ 1 can enchilada sauce
- ☐ 1 can black olives

Dairy
- ☐ 1 pkg. 4oz. Feta cheese
- ☐ 1 qt. milk
- ☐ 1 container strawberry cream cheese fruit dip
- ☐ 8 oz. tub whipped topping
- ☐ 2 cups shredded cheese
- ☐ small sour cream

Frozen
- ☐ 1 pkg. mixed veggies
- ☐ 1 pkg. frozen tator tots
- ☐ 1 pkg. frozen peas and carrots

Spice List
- ☐ oregano
- ☐ basil
- ☐ salt and pepper
- ☐ Worcestershire sauce
- ☐ cider vinegar small bottle
- ☐ chili powder
- ☐ garlic powder
- ☐ dry mustard
- ☐ ground cumin
- ☐ celery flakes
- ☐ parsley flakes
- ☐ salsa

Other Stuff
- ☐ brown sugar
- ☐ 1 dozen sandwich rolls
- ☐ 1 tube refrigerated sugar cookie dough
- ☐ 2 pkg. refrigerated biscuits
- ☐ 6 oz. graham cracker crust
- ☐ 6 flour tortillas

Add Your Own Items:

THE RUSH HOUR COOK

PRESTO PASTA
by Brook Noel

THE TALES AND RECIPES OF A CORPORATE WOMAN TACKLING TODAY'S KITCHEN

CHAMPION PRESS LTD.
Milwaukee, Wisconsin

Dedication

THIS ONE IS FOR THE CREW...

FOR MICHAEL... WHO NEVER FAILS TO KEEP A SMILE ON HIS FACE AND A GOOD WORD ON HIS TONGUE, EVEN WHEN HE'S LAYING OUT THE 18-ZILLIONTH COOKBOOK OF THE WEEK. THANK YOU FOR YOUR LAUGHTER!

FOR JOAN... WHO MULTI-TASKS BETTER THAN ANY MANIC WOMAN I HAVE SEEN TO DATE-WHILE KEEPING HER COOL. THANK YOU FOR YOUR INNOVATIVENESS AND JUGGLING SKILLS! (YOU'RE WONDERFUL-NOW IF I COULD JUST GET YOU OFF THOSE TOFU-BROCCOLI SANDWICHES...)

FOR CRAIG... WHO GREETS EVERY DAY LIKE A TRUE CHAMPION. THANK YOU FOR YOUR ATTENTION TO DETAIL, THOROUGHNESS AND FUN SPIRIT.

FOR WENDY... WHO WATCHES OVER ALL OUR MANUSCRIPTS AND ENDEAVORS WITH EYES LIKE A HAWK. THANK YOU FOR YOUR DEDICATION.

FOR SARA ... WHO INSPIRES, HELPS AND ASSISTS IN MANY-A-WAYS.

AND LAST, BUT OF COURSE, NOT LEAST-FOR MARY ANN WHO MANAGES TO KEEP MY LIFE FLOWING SMOOTHLY WHILE TAKING CARE OF ALL OUR CHAMPIONS. THANK YOU FOR ALL YOU DO.

THE RUSH HOUR COOK ~ 4

PRESTO PASTA

Contents

IN THE BEGINNING...
SOUPS, SIDES & STARTERS

Bedazzling Breadsticks	14
Turkey Noodle Soup	14
Tossed Italiano Saladio	15
Garlic Bread	15
Creamy Italian Dressing	16
Fresh Bruschetta	16
Pepper Pasta Salad	17
Minestrone in a Minute	18
Chicken Noodle Zupa	19
Rockin' Rotini	20
Special Spaetzle	20

A MERRY MIDDLE...
MAIN MEALS IN MINUTES

Tantalizing Turkey Dijon	23
Easy Cheese Pasta	24
Hammy Noodles	24
No Red-Sauce Spaghetti	25
Awesomely Easy Alfredo	25
This Ain't Your Mother's Ravioli	26
M&M Pasta	27
Fettuccini ala Ham	27
Spaghetti Pie	28
Baked Ziti Con Queso	29
Skinny Alfredo	30
Presto Mac	31
Chicken and Veggie Pasta	32
Chicken Tetrazzini	33
Greek Spaghetti Sauce	34
Chicken Parmesan	35
Zesty Ziti	35
Skimpy Scampi	36
Rite-a-Way Ramen Noodles	37
Bowtie Bonanza	38
Sea Shells	40
Time Out Tuna Casserole	41
Late from Work Lasagna	42

Light and Easy Pasta Toss	43
Spaghetti-O-No It's Dinner Time	43
Italian Pasta Skillet	44
Almost Oriental Noodle Dish	44
Chicken and Ravioli	45
Parmesan Rotini	45
Magnificent Mac	46
Chicken Noodle Casserole	46

A Sweet & Happy Ending... Delectable Desserts

Cinnamon Donuts in a Jiffy	48
Strawberry Sundaes	48
Tear-It-Up Tiramisu	49

Etcetera...

A Few Things You'll Need to Know	7
Producing Pasta Presto	9
The Five Rules	12
Plate Prep	17
Pasta Defined	19
Pesto Magic	23
Creative Combos	26
Quick-Cooking Pasta	27
Pasta Bake	30
3 Steps to Perfect Pasta	34
Pasta Equivalents	38
Does Pasta = Pounds	39
Personal Shopper – List # 1	52
Personal Shopper – List # 2	55
Personal Shopper – List # 3	58

A Few Things You'll Need to Know...

Pay close attention when you see this symbol. It means that you are about to uncover a 'Mother-Knows-Best' tip which will save you countless headaches when feeding your children.

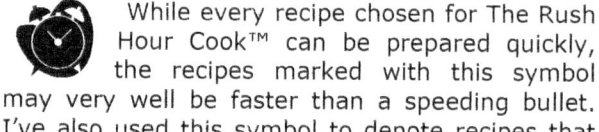

While every recipe chosen for The Rush Hour Cook™ can be prepared quickly, the recipes marked with this symbol may very well be faster than a speeding bullet. I've also used this symbol to denote recipes that save valuable time or offer make-ahead options.

At the end of this book, you'll find a section called, Your Personal Shopper. I've included pre-planned menus and grocery lists to get you through those rough weeks when you don't feel like planning - which is just about every week, for me! These are the recipes that I now use much to my family's satisfaction and success.

PRESTO PASTA

Serve It Up—All recipes are sized for 6 Servings, unless otherwise noted. If you have a family of 3 or 4, consider adding a few more members or better yet, make the full recipe anyway. Use the rest for lunches the following day, or freeze these extras as healthy, homemade options to those ready-made, chemical-laden convenience-meals.

High-fat, some-fat, low-fat or no-fat—Most of the recipes within this book are either low in fat or easily adaptable for low fat options. When prepared this way, the caloric and fat intakes coincide with each meal containing less than 30% fat.

Make Your Misto™— In most cookbooks, almost every recipe calls for cooking spray. Instead of using the aerosol cans that you can buy in the store, purchase a Misto™ or other non-aerosol pump. With these pumps, you can add a bit of olive, canola or vegetable oil and they will convert the oil to spray. This allows you to use the minimum amount of oil and avoid the nasty-chemicals found in their store-shelved counter-parts.

Producing Presto Pasta

So far, each Rush Hour™ volume has begun with some silly story or tale from my past cooking experiences. While all the topics came naturally, I found myself stumped on what to write about pasta. I sat at the table in my mom's house, drumming my pen. "I just don't have anything to write about..." I sighed.

"What about the bouillon story?" she asked.

"That's not funny—that could have happened to anyone."

She cast a quizzical glance. "What about the story where you turned the pizza into a lasagna?"

"Well that could have happened to anyone, too..." I offered in defense. The stories seemed more sad to me than funny, but she assured me there was some humor there. I'll let you be the judge.

The Story of the Bad Bouillon

When my husband and I first married I thought it would be nice to learn to cook. He had grown up in a family where he was used to homemade meals and family dinners. In the single parent-household where I grew up, we often ate on the run. So anyway, one of his favorite dishes was-beef stroganoff. How hard could it be? I thought. Noodles + beef, must = stroganoff. Deciding nothing could be that easy, I resorted to a cookbook's advice. I quickly compiled a list of ingredients, noticing a substance called "bouillon." While I hadn't heard of bouillon, since it sort of rhymed with onion. I presumed it was a vegetable.

Off I went in the supermarket, manically pushing my cart and corralling my ingredients. It took only moments to gather beef, noodles... and then the final item came: BOUILLON. I swerved over to the vegetable aisle and started digging amongst the bean sprouts, ginger, garlic and green onions. Nothing. Like a man too proud to ask for directions, I watched the store stockers go by and did not seek their help in my search. Frustrated and bouillon-less I slowly steered my cart for an alternative aisle. While wandering aimlessly, I passed the soups. Then I saw it. There amongst the red and white cans was a soup named "beef bouillon." I tossed it in my cart and raced for the express lane.

Back at the ranch I heated my pans, boiled my noodles and followed the directions to a tee. When I got to adding the bouillon it seemed a bit suspect. It suggested I add "two cubes." I turned to the metric equivalency chart, but alas, there weren't any conversion numbers for cube. I poured the equivalent of two ice cube tray indents into my mixture. Needless to say it turned out quite bland.

The Saga of the Pizz-agna

And then, of course, there was the pizza turned lasagna. How was I to know that not every pizza can be microwaved successfully? I tossed the pizza into the microwave for 10 minutes. With pizza cutter in hand, I pulled it from the microwave. Drat, I had forgotten to remove the plastic. I grabbed my other pizza from the freezer and removed the plastic, tossing it to the same fate of the microwave.

Another beep. I opened the door and was amazed by what I found. There sat a circular shape that had once resembled a pizza and now resembled a soupy like flood of sauces and cheese. "Hmmmm..." I thought. "What to do..." A light bulb went on. I carefully removed the droopy bread and saucy stuff from the microwave and tossed it in a casserole dish. Many of the colors were similar to those found in lasagna. I grabbed a spoon, broke it up and mixed well. Then I topped it with a disguise of mozzarella cheese. After thirty minutes in a 350 degree oven, I announced that dinner was served.

"Hmm... what's this?" my husband asked. I think he was impressed by the beautiful looking dish. I had added a few sprigs of parsley for garnish.

"Lasagna," I replied excitedly, knowing it was his favorite dish.

After serving us each a chunk, my husband looked at me somewhat puzzled. "Interesting texture," he announced. I watched him chew, not yet brave enough to try it myself. "There seems to be..." he paused, "bread in it." He smiled broadly. "Isn't the bread normally served on the side, honey?"

Needless to say, after these two incidents, my husband suddenly started eating "big lunches" at work and wasn't hungry for my different homemade preparations. Of course all that is changing—little did he know that he had married The Rush Hour Cook™ in the Making.

While far from an expert, I have successfully tackled the kitchen to bring tasty, healthy meals to my family's dinner table at mock 10 speed. I am the owner of a fast-growing publishing company and my husband is an executive officer for a software company. Our manic schedules of work and travel have taught me that if we don't connect over the dinner hour, we may not connect all day. While that was fine when it was just he and I, we now have a seven-year-old daughter, and realize how important the family dinner hour has become. The recipes I found are not only foolproof, but can be prepared quickly and enjoyed by the pickiest of eaters. To choose recipes for this series, I followed five guidelines, which you'll find on the following page.

The Five Rules of Rush Hour Recipes:

1. All ingredients should be able to be pronounced accurately through the phonetic use of the English Language.

2. Each ingredient can be located in the market without engaging in a full scale scavenger hunt.

3. No list of ingredients shall be longer than the instructions.

4. Each recipe has to be durable enough to survive me, the Queen-of-Incapable-Cooking, and elicit a compliment at meal's end.

5. My finicky child will eat it—or some portion of it. I've learned not to be too picky on this one. I'll often break out part of the recipe and prepare it separately to her liking.

So without further adieu, let's get cooking! (I promise I didn't even include my "pizza-lasagna" recipe!)

In the Beginning...
Soups, Sides & Starters

Quick Recipe Index:

Bedazzling Breadsticks	14
Turkey Noodle Soup	14
Tossed Italiano Saladio	15
Garlic Bread	15
Creamy Italian Dressing	16
Fresh Bruschetta	16
Pepper Pasta Salad	17
Minestrone in a Minute	18
Chicken Noodle Zupa	19
Rockin' Rotini	20
Special Spaetzle	20

Bedazzling Breadsticks

1 can refrigerated biscuits
1 tablespoon garlic powder
2 tablespoons butter or margarine, melted
sesame seeds*
poppy seeds*
dried minced onion*

Roll biscuits in hands to create breadsticks about 6 inches long. Mix garlic powder and melted butter in small bowl and brush on breadsticks. Bake according to package directions. Top with optional items.*

Turkey Noodle Soup

3 cups chicken broth
2¼ cups water
1½ cups chopped cooked turkey (or chicken)
1 cup thinly sliced carrots
½ cup thinly sliced celery
¼ teaspoon pepper
½ teaspoon onion powder
2 cups dried wide noodles

In a large saucepan combine the chicken broth, water, meat, carrots, celery and seasonings. Bring to a boil and then reduce heat and simmer for 12-15 minutes. Add noodles and cook uncovered until tender.

Tossed Italiano Saladio
(also known as The Pizza Salad)

1 bunch Romaine lettuce, torn
turkey pepperoni
mozzarella cheese
black olives
onion
mushrooms
green pepper
tomatoes
Italian dressing

It doesn't get any easier than this. Toss all of the above and enjoy. Sometimes the simple is overlooked.

Garlic Bread

1 loaf French bread
1 stick butter or margarine, melted
2 tablespoons garlic powder
2 tablespoons fresh minced parsley
1 tablespoon oregano

Cut loaf in half. Mix butter and spices and spread over bread. Bake at 450 degrees for 10 to 15 minutes until golden brown and bubbly.

PRESSED FOR TIME?
TRY RICE NOODLES. THESE TERRIFIC TIMESAVERS DON'T NEED TO BE COOKED— SIMPLY LET THEM STAND IN WARM WATER FOR A FEW MOMENTS AND THEY ARE GOOD TO GO.

Creamy Italian Dressing

1 cup mayonnaise
2 tablespoons grated Parmesan cheese
2 tablespoons red wine vinegar
2 teaspoons sugar
1 teaspoon Italian seasoning or ½ teaspoon basil and ½ teaspoon oregano
½ teaspoon salt
½ teaspoon garlic pepper
3-4 tablespoons milk

Combine all ingredients except for milk. Chill for a minimum of two hours. Before serving add milk to create desired consistency.

Fresh Bruschetta

1 mini loaf of French bread cut into ¾" slices
¼ cup olive or favorite flavored oil
2 fresh tomatoes diced
1 tablespoon minced garlic
2 tablespoons chopped fresh basil
1 tablespoon chopped fresh parsley
1 tablespoon fresh oregano
1 teaspoon olive oil
(note: can be made with dried spices but tastes much better with fresh)

Preheat oven to 375 degrees. Place bread on ungreased cookie sheet. Drizzle oil over bread. Bake about 8-10 minutes. While bread is baking mix diced tomatoes with spices and 1 teaspoon olive oil. When bread is done, top with tomato mixture and serve immediately.

> I REALIZE THAT ALL OF THE SIDE DISHES IN THIS SECTION DON'T CONTAIN PASTA- HOWEVER, EACH MAKE PERFECT ACCOMPANIMENTS AND MAN CANNOT SURVIVE ON PASTA ALONE!

Pepper Pasta Salad

1 (12 oz.) package rotini pasta
1 green pepper, julienned
1 yellow pepper, julienned
1 red pepper, julienned
1 (4 ½ oz.) jar whole mushrooms, halved
1 (6 oz.) jar pitted black olives, halved
½ cup julienned red onion
¾ cup Italian dressing
¼ teaspoon salt
½ teaspoon pepper
12-oz. mozzarella cheese, cubed

Cook rotini according to package directions and drain. Combine peppers, mushrooms, black olives, and red onion in bowl. Add drained pasta to veggies. In a small bowl, mix dressing, salt and pepper. Add Mozzarella cheese and dressing mixture to veggie/pasta mixture and toss. Refrigerate for one hour minimum prior to serving. Can be made 24 hours in advance. If salad seems dry, add more Italian dressing right before serving. (note: make sure pasta has cooled before adding to the salad)

> **PLATE PREP**
> IT'S A GOOD IDEA TO HEAT YOUR SERVING DISHES BEFORE PLACING PASTA IN THEM. USE A 200 DEGREE OVEN AND HEAT DISHES 5-10 MINUTES TO HELP MAINTAIN GREAT TASTE AND MAXIMUM FLAVOR.

Minestrone in a Minute

1 pound frozen Italian veggies(carrots, Italian green beans, and cauliflower
1 cup water
1 can lima beans drained
1 (14.5 oz.) can chopped Italian tomatoes
1 small can tomato paste
2 cans beef broth
1 can kidney beans
1 small onion, chopped
1 zucchini, chopped or sliced
1 tablespoon oregano
1 tablespoon thyme
2 cups elbow macaroni, cooked

Put all ingredients in a large stock pot or 5 quart pot except for the cooked pasta. Simmer for 30 minutes. Add pasta and cook for 10 minutes. If desired to turn into a main dish meal, add chopped sirloin or other leftover beef.

Chicken Noodle Zupa

2 pounds chopped cooked chicken
2 cans chicken broth
2 tablespoons parsley
1 teaspoon salt
½ teaspoon pepper
1 bay leaf
2 onions, chopped
1 cup chopped celery
1 cup frozen peas
2 cups sliced carrots
½ cup water
2 tablespoons flour
3 cups dried wide egg noodles, cooked

In a large stockpot, add 1 tablespoon oil. Sauté celery, onions and carrots until soft, but still crunchy, over medium low heat. Stir frequently. Add all remaining ingredients except the water, flour and noodles. Simmer the chicken vegetable mixture over low heat, covered, for about 30 minutes. In a separate dish blend the water and flour, then add to the soup, stirring constantly to thicken. Add cooked egg noodles and simmer uncovered for 10 minutes more.

Pesto Defined

As I was attempting to create these many pasta dishes I kept running into one ingredient that especially stumped me... PESTO. Many recipes called for PESTO but no one told me what it was-or how to make it! So if you are in the dark about pesto, fear not-I shall shed some light. Pesto is fresh basil, olive oil, garlic, sharply flavored cheese and pine nuts all mixed into one great concoction. Many have called it "the taste of Italy!"

Rockin' Rotini

12 ounces tri-colored rotini pasta
1 cup deli salami, diced
1 cup provolone cheese, diced
1 cup fat-free Italian salad dressing

Cook rotini according to package directions, drain and rinse with cold water. Add all other ingredients. Cover and refrigerate until serving.

Special Spaetzle

1 cup all-purpose flour
⅛ teaspoon salt
1 beaten egg
⅓ cup milk
1 tablespoon margarine or butter
3 tablespoons fine dry bread crumbs

Stir flour and salt together in a large mixing bowl. In a small mixing bowl stir together egg and milk. Add smaller bowl's contents to large bowl and mix to finish off batter. Bring a large pot of water to a boil. Place colander with large holes over water. Place batter into colander and push through holes with hands or spatula forming small pieces. Cook for 5 to 10 minutes or until spaetzle are tender but still firm. Drain. Melt margarine or butter; toss with bread crumbs and sprinkle over spaetzle.

A Merry Middle...
Main Meals in Minutes

Quick Recipe Index:

Tantalizing Turkey Dijon	23
Easy Cheese Pasta	24
Hammy Noodles	24
No Red-Sauce Spaghetti	25
Awesomely Easy Alfredo	25
This Ain't Your Mother's Ravioli	26
M&M Pasta	27
Fettuccini ala Ham	27
Spaghetti Pie	28
Baked Ziti Con Queso	29
Skinny Alfredo	30
Presto Mac	31
Chicken and Veggie Pasta	32
Chicken Tetrazzini	33
Greek Spaghetti Sauce	34
Chicken Parmesan	35
Zesty Ziti	35
Skimpy Scampi	36
Rite-a-Way Ramen Noodles	37
Bowtie Bonanza	38
Sea Shells	40
Time Out Tuna Casserole	41
Late from Work Lasagna	42
Light and Easy Pasta Toss	43
Spaghetti-O-No It's Dinner Time	43
Italian Pasta Skillet	44
Almost Oriental Noodle Dish	44

Chicken and Ravioli	45
Parmesan Rotini	45
Magnificent Mac	46
Chicken Noodle Casserole	46

Tantalizing Turkey Dijon

12 oz. fettuccini
1 clove garlic, minced
1 teaspoon Italian seasoning
½ cup butter
3 cups turkey, cooked and chopped into
   bite sized pieces
⅓ cup Dijon-style mustard

Cook pasta according to package directions, drain and set aside. In a small saucepan melt butter and add Italian seasoning, garlic and mustard. Stir in turkey and cook for 2 minutes to blend flavors. Serve immediately over cooked pasta.

Parents: Divide the butter/turkey mixture in half and add fresh or frozen vegetables to your portion to jazz it up. Or leave all the mixture in one pan adding only those vegetables that are "childproof", in other words, edible at your home.

MAKE A LITTLE PESTO MAGIC
TAKE SOME OF YOUR PESTO (SEE PAGE 19) AND MIX IT WITH SOFT BUTTER FOR A DELICIOUS TREAT ON WARM BREAD. THAT'S SURE TO IMPRESS FELLOW DINERS.

PRESTO PASTA

Easy Cheese Pasta

1 (16 oz.) package small pasta (penne, spiral, wagon wheel, elbow—whatever your pantry contains is perfect)
1 stick butter (or margarine)
1 cup shredded Swiss cheese
1 cup shredded Parmesan cheese
1-2 tablespoons milk (if needed)

Cook pasta according to package directions, drain and rinse with cold water. Melt butter in a small sauce pan. Add pasta and cheese to pan, cooking until the cheese has just melted. Add a touch of milk to thin the cheese if desired.

Hammy Noodles

¾ pound ham, diced
1½ cups shredded cheese (you choose the type: Parmesan, mozzarella, Swiss or cheddar)
1½ cups light cream
1¼ pound linguine
salt and pepper

Cook pasta according to package directions. Rinse and drain. Warm cream over low heat. Once hot, add ham and continue cooking for 10 minutes, stirring frequently. Do not boil. Add cheese. Stir until melted. Mix sauce with pasta in a serving bowl. Tada!

No-Red-Sauce Spaghetti

Makes 4 servings

1 pound spaghetti
½ pound bacon, diced
½ pound pre-sliced pepperoni, cut in halves
½ cup frozen peas
½ cup frozen corn

Cook bacon and pepperoni over medium heat until bacon is crisp. Cook pasta according to package directions, drain. Cook vegetables according to package directions, drain. Mix all together and serve.

Awesomely Easy Alfredo

Makes 4 servings

¼ cup room temperature half and half
1 tablespoon margarine or butter
3 oz. packaged fettuccine, linguine or similar pasta
½ cup frozen peas
¼ cup Parmesan cheese, grated
½ teaspoon finely shredded lemon peel

Cook fettuccini according to package directions, but add the peas during the last five minutes of cooking. Drain. Return to pan. Add remaining ingredients and stir until heated through.

This Ain't Your Mother's Ravioli

9 oz. ground round
12 oz. soft-style cream cheese
30 wonton wrappers
2¼ cups prepared spaghetti sauce

In a bowl stir together ground round and cream cheese. Place a spoonful of filling in the center of each wrapper. Brush wrapper edges with water. Fold corner to corner to form triangle shape and press edges together. Drop into boiling water and cook for 3-5 minutes or until meat is done. Heat sauce in a separate saucepan. Top ravioli with sauce.

Variations:

Try diced ham and cheese topped with store-bought Alfredo sauce (like Five Brothers™) or diced vegetables topped with teriyaki sauce. The possibilities are endless. Don't forget to freeze extra ravioli for a quick made-ahead meal. And of course, if worse comes to worse, there are all those pre-packaged refrigerated raviolis nowadays...I won't tell if you won't!

M&M Pasta

8 oz. dried pasta such as ziti, rigatoni
   or mostaccioli
12 oz. fresh Italian sausage links, sliced
30 oz. spaghetti sauce
½ cup half and half

Cook pasta according to package directions, drain. In 2-quart saucepan cook sliced sausage over medium heat until cooked through, turning frequently. Drain well. Add spaghetti sauce to sausage and bring just to boiling. Stir in cream; heat through. Toss with pasta and top with Parmesan cheese, if desired.

QUICK-COOKING PASTA
ANGEL HAIR PASTA IS ONE OF THE QUICKEST COOKING NOODLES. JUST 3-4 MINUTES AND YOU'RE GOOD TO GO! KEEP SOME ON HAND FOR QUICK-DINNER FIXES.

Fettuccini a la Ham

18 oz. evaporated skim milk
3 teaspoons cornstarch
½ teaspoon dry mustard
½ cup shredded Swiss cheese
1½ cups sliced fully cooked ham, cut into
   bite-size strips (about 5 oz.)
1 (2½ oz.) jar sliced mushrooms, optional
4 cups cooked fettuccini

Stir milk, cornstarch and mustard over medium heat until thickened and bubbly. Add cheese and stir until melted. Last but not least, add the ham (and the drained mushrooms—if you dare!) Serve over fettuccini.

Spaghetti Pie

6 oz. dry spaghetti noodles
2 tablespoons margarine
½ cup Parmesan cheese
2 eggs, beaten
1 teaspoon vegetable oil
½ cup onion, chopped
1 (16 oz.) can Italian-style stewed
   tomatoes, undrained
1 (6 oz.) can tomato paste
1 teaspoon sugar
1 teaspoon oregano
½ clove garlic, minced
1 cup fat-free cottage cheese
½ cup reduced-fat cheddar cheese, grated

Chop onion. Mince garlic. Cook spaghetti noodles according to package directions. Drain. Stir margarine into hot noodles until melted. Stir in Parmesan cheese and beaten eggs. Spray 9-inch pie plate with cooking spray. Form pasta mixture into a crust-shape in bottom and up sides of pie plate. Store covered in refrigerator until ready to use. Then, in a skillet, heat vegetable oil. Cook onion until softened. Add tomatoes, tomato paste, sugar, oregano and garlic. Heat through. Spread cottage cheese over bottom of spaghetti crust. Top with tomato mixture. Sprinkle grated cheese over all and bake for 20 minuets in 350 degree oven. You can also make an extra pie or two and freeze them for later use. Simply top with foil and adjust your cooking time to 25 minutes covered, 5 uncovered.
*From Frozen Assets Lite and Easy
by Deborah Taylor-Hough*

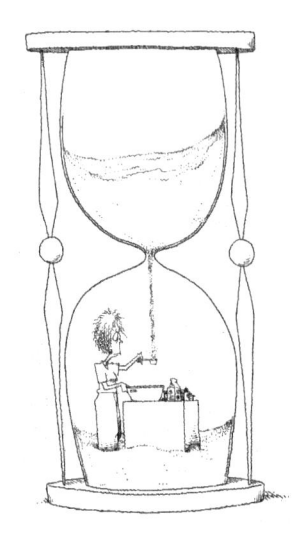

THE RUSH HOUR COOK ~ 28

PRESTO PASTA

Baked Ziti Con Queso

2 tablespoons olive oil
1 onion, chopped
2 large garlic cloves, pressed
⅓ cup tomato paste
1 (8 oz.) can tomato sauce
1 cup water
1 teaspoon oregano, crumbled
½ teaspoon sage
½ cup grated Romano cheese
1 (15-oz) container ricotta cheese
1 egg
8 oz. mozzarella cheese, grated
1 pound cooked ziti or other tubular pasta

Preheat oven to 425 degrees. Lightly grease a 9 x 13 baking dish. Cook onion and garlic over low heat until soft. Mix in tomato paste and cook another minute. Add tomato sauce, water, oregano and sage. Simmer until mixture thickens slightly, about 10 minutes. Stir in ¼ cup Romano cheese, and salt and pepper to taste. In a medium bowl combine ricotta cheese and egg. Reserve ¼ cup mozzarella cheese for topping. Add remaining mozzarella to ricotta cheese mixture and blend. Now put this thing together like a lasagna. Start with the tomato sauce on the bottom of the baking dish. Next, layer ⅓ of the pasta. Drop half of ricotta cheese mixture over by the spoonful. Then put the sauce on , etc. Top with remaining mozzarella cheese and bake for 30 to 40 minutes. – From the Frantic Family Cookbook by Leanne Ely

---

YOUR POT NEED NOT RUNNETH OVER

ADD A TABLESPOON OF VEGETABLE OIL TO YOUR BOILING WATER TO PREVENT THE DREADED "LOOK I MADE A FLOWING FOUNTAIN OUT OF MY STOVE" SYNDROME AS WELL AS STICKY NOODLES.

Skinny Alfredo

Makes 4 servings

1 (12 oz.) package fettuccine noodles
3 tablespoons margarine
1 tablespoon flour
½ cup skim milk (or 1%)
½ cup Parmesan cheese
salt and pepper to taste
4 skinless, boneless chicken breasts, diced

Cook fettuccine according to package directions. Drain well. Place in a large bowl and keep warm. Boil or grill chicken breasts and then cut up and add to the fettuccine. In another pan, melt butter and add flour. Stir until smooth. Cook for 3 to 4 minutes, stirring constantly. Gradually add milk. Turn heat up to medium and continue stirring until mixture is thick and bubbly. Reduce heat to low and stir in Parmesan cheese. Cook until cheese dissolves and mixture is smooth. Pour sauce over fettuccine and toss gently to coat. Serve with a tossed salad and herb sticks or garlic bread.

> **PASTA BAKE:** IF YOU ARE PREPARING PASTA THAT WILL BE USED IN A BAKED-DISH, UNDERCOOK IT FOR A FEW MINUTES SO THAT IT WILL COMPLETE ITS COOKING CYCLE DURING THE BAKING PROCESS.

Presto Mac

1 pound dried elbow macaroni
⅓ cup butter or margarine
2 cups shredded cheddar cheese
½ cup bread crumbs
3 large eggs
2 cups milk
¼ teaspoon pepper
¼ teaspoon salt

Cook macaroni just until tender. Drain. Return macaroni to pan, add butter and ¾ cup cheese and stir. Spray a casserole dish with cooking spray. Sprinkle cheese and ½ of the bread crumbs on bottom of casserole dish. Combine eggs, milk, salt and pepper in a bowl Add to macaroni and stir well. Transfer mixture to casserole dish. Top with remaining cheese and breadcrumbs. Bake in a 400 degree oven for 15-20 minutes.

> TO CREATE PERFECT PASTA, USE 4-6 QUARTS OF COLD WATER, HEATED TO A FULL BOIL FOR A POUND OF DRY PASTA. IT'S IMPORTANT TO HAVE ENOUGH WATER TO LET THE PASTA HAVE "ROOM" TO COOK. ONCE YOU ADD THE PASTA, RETURN IT TO A FULL BOIL BEFORE STARTING TO "TIME" YOUR DINNER. WHEN DONE, DRAIN IN A COLANDER AND MIX IMMEDIATELY WITH THE SERVING SAUCE

PRESTO PASTA

Chicken & Veggie Pasta

1 (8 oz.) package curly pasta
1 head broccoli
1 head cauliflower
3 boneless skinless chicken
   breasts, cubed
½ cup Parmesan cheese
¼ cup margarine or butter

Make pasta according to the package directions. Drain. Cut up veggies and steam in microwave (approximately 5-7 minutes). Sauté chicken breast pieces until cooked all the way through. Melt butter in pan with chicken and toss in veggies and Parmesan cheese. Pour over cooked pasta. Serve with a salad and crusty bread.

> **COLOR YOUR WORLD**
> LOOKING FOR A FUN WAY TO SERVE PASTA? ADD COLOR! SIMPLY PLACE A FEW DROPS OF FOOD COLORING IN YOUR COOKING WATER. TRY RED AND GREEN FOR THE HOLIDAYS. KIDS ALSO LOVE TO PICK THEIR PASTA COLOR AND SHAPE.

PRESTO PASTA

Chicken Tetrazzini

4 whole skinless chicken breasts
2 cans cream of chicken soup
1 can cream of mushroom soup
1 cup milk
1 cup water
1 tablespoon dried minced onion
2 cups shredded cheddar cheese
1 package (8 oz.) spaghetti pasta or other shaped pasta
2 teaspoons parsley flakes
2 teaspoons basil
1 tablespoon Worcestershire Sauce
1 cup sour cream or plain yogurt
1 teaspoon salt
½ teaspoon coarse black pepper

Place chicken breasts in crockpot. Cover with cream of chicken soup and 1 cup water. Cover with lid and cook on high for 6 hours. Remove chicken and cut into bite-sized pieces. Return chicken to crockpot. Add all remaining ingredients except pasta and cheese. Cover crockpot and reduce heat to low. Continue cooking for 1-3 hours. About 30 minutes prior to serving, stir in sour cream. In separate saucepan, prepare pasta according to package directions. Cook until tender, but firm. Rinse and drain. Serve crockpot mixture over pasta. Top with shredded cheese.

PRESTO PASTA

Greek Spaghetti Sauce

1 lb. lean ground beef
2 tablespoons olive oil
1 large clove garlic, minced
½ cup red wine or sherry
1 (1lb.) can stewed tomatoes
1 (6 oz) can tomato paste
2-inch stick of cinnamon, broken
8-10 whole cloves
1 teaspoon salt
½ teaspoon pepper

Brown meat and minced garlic in olive oil and then drain on a paper towel or brown paper when meat is fully cooked through. Tie spices in a bag of cheesecloth. Combine all ingredients in crockpot and add 1 tomato paste can of water. Cover with lid and cook on low for 5 hours. For a thicker sauce cook on high for 8 hours, removing the lid after the firs 2-3 hours of cooking time. Serve over cooked pasta. *From Crazy About Crockpots by Penny E. Stone*

STEP 1 TO PERFECT PASTA: USE AT LEAST A QUART OF WATER FOR EVERY 4 OUNCES OF PASTA.

STEP 2 TO PERFECT PASTA: BRING WATER TO A FAST BOIL. BE SURE THE WATER REMAINS BOILING AT ALL TIMES.

STEP 3 TO PERFECT PASTA: STIR FREQUENTLY FOR EVEN COOKING.

Chicken Parmesan

Makes 4 servings

4 skinless, boneless chicken breasts
½ cup flour
1 tablespoon oregano
1 tablespoon garlic, if desired
½ cup Parmesan cheese, divided
1 jar meatless spaghetti sauce
1 (8 oz.) package , mozzarella cheese
4 cups cooked pasta, any kind

Preheat oven to 375 degrees. Mix flour, oregano, garlic and ¼ cup of the Parmesan cheese in a shallow bowl then coat chicken and cook till browned on both sides. Cover with sauce and remaining ¼ cup of Parmesan cheese and cook for 30 minutes. Uncover and top with mozzarella cheese and cook for an additional 10 minutes or until bubbly. Serve with whatever pasta is in the pantry.

Zesty Ziti

Makes 4 servings

1 pound Ziti
1 lb. chopped, cooked chicken
2 tsp. margarine
1 onion, chopped
2 tablespoons flour
1 tablespoon Dijon mustard
2 cups chicken broth
¼ cup lemon juice
1 (10-oz.) package frozen peas

Prepare pasta according to package directions. While pasta is cooking, defrost peas. Warm the butter or margarine over medium heat in a large skillet. Add the onion and cook for 3 minutes. Stir in the Dijon mustard and flour. Very gradually whisk in the chicken broth. Bring the broth to a boil and stir in the lemon juice, peas and parsley. When pasta is done, drain it well. Toss pasta and cooked chicken with sauce, season with salt and pepper and serve.

Skimpy Scampi

2 pounds peeled and de-veined fresh shrimp
½ cup cooking wine (dry white is best)
2 tablespoons minced garlic
¼ cup flour
1 tablespoon chopped parsley
½ cup butter or margarine
16 oz. cooked fettuccine noodles
Parmesan, to serve on the side

NOTE: I call this Skimpy Scampi since the kids would likely forego the first 6 ingredients and just take the last two. So while their serving might be a bit Skimpy... try the full recipe to reward yourself with tasty Scampi.

Rinse shrimp and dip in flour. Melt butter in pan and add garlic. Sauté shrimp in butter mixture until opaque and lightly browned. About 2 minutes on each side. Add wine and cook for 3 minutes over medium heat (watch your eyebrows since this might flame up due to the alcohol). Toss shrimp and butter mixture with parsley and pour over fettuccine. Serve with Parmesan cheese an the side.

> *NEVER WASTE A NOODLE AGAIN*
>
> DID YOU KNOW THAT YOU CAN EASILY REHEAT PASTA? HERE'S THE TRICK... COOK TWICE WHAT YOU NEED. IMMEDIATELY RINSE THE EXTRA IN COLD WATER, SHAKING WELL WITH A COLANDER. PLACE THE EXTRA PASTA IN A BOWL AND TOSS WITH ONE TABLESPOON VEGETABLE OIL. REFRIGERATE. TO REHEAT, DROP THE PASTA INTO BOILING WATER FOR ONE MINUTE, OR UNTIL HEATED THROUGH.

Rite-a-Way Ramen™ Noodles

Makes 4 servings

2 packages chicken Ramen™ noodles
1 package frozen mixed vegetables
1 tablespoon soy sauce
1½ cup water

Gently break apart noodles. Stir noodles, seasoning packets, mixed veggies, soy sauce and water in a sauce pan. Boil 3-4 minutes. Okay, so this isn't going to make it on the Food Network™ but it's fast, easy and ridiculously inexpensive. Talk about a desperation dinner that even the kids will eat. If you want, add 1 cup of protein such as diced cooked chicken for a heartier meal.

Bowtie Bonanza

Makes 4 servings

4 cups dried bow tie pasta
2 cups fresh or frozen asparagus, cooked
¼ pound ham julienned
1 (8 oz.) package cream cheese, softened
1 tablespoon oregano
1 tablespoon garlic
⅓ cup milk
10 cherry tomatoes, halved
¼ cup Parmesan cheese, if desired

Make pasta according to package directions. While pasta is cooking, simmer asparagus 'til tender. In a small bowl mix softened cream cheese with spices and milk. In a skillet heated over medium low heat (sprayed with cooking spray) toss pasta, asparagus, ham and cream cheese mixing 'til warm and bubbly. Stir constantly so that sauce doesn't scorch. Right before serving add tomatoes and Parmesan cheese if desired. Viola! Enjoy!

Pasta Equivalents

Do you end up with too much pasta or not enough? Use the chart below to take the mystery out of measuring.

Size	Uncooked	Cooked
Small to Medium	8 oz.	4 cups
Large	8 oz. or 1½ inch diameter bunch	4 cups
Egg Noodles	8 oz.	2 ½ cups

SOURCE: The National Pasta Association. Check their site for everything you could ever want to know about noodles…. and then some! www.ilovepasta.org

Does Pasta = Pounds?

Despite the carbo-warnings, pasta remains a favorite staple of low-fat diets. The USDA's Handbook sites a 1/2 cup serving of cooked pasta (spaghetti) contains a mere 99 calories, less than half a gram of fat, and less than 5 milligrams of sodium. Of course, whole-wheat pasta is the best choice-and definitely worth a taste test.

The danger with weight gain comes when we use a rich sauce. To keep your pasta dishes high-flavor yet low-fat, follow these simple guidelines:

~ Stay away from white sauces-especially pre-purchased ones. Instead try low-fat milk, fat-free sour cream, non-fat yogurt, fat-free mayo, and evaporated milk as main ingredients for cream sauces

~ Make extra tomato and vegetable-based sauces to have on hand.

~ Resist the temptation to always add meat to a pasta dish. Try adding beans, lentils or additional vegetables.

~ Experiment with herbs and spices and enjoy their added flavor.

~ When using cheese, opt for a little and add more as desired. Try using sharp cheddar for flavor. Often you can use less of a stronger cheese and still get the same flavor as its milder counterpart.

Sea Shells

12 uncooked jumbo pasta shells
1 (8 oz.) container ricotta cheese
1 (8 oz.) package mozzarella cheese
¼ cup Parmesan cheese
1 egg
1 tablespoon fresh parsley
1 tablespoon oregano
1 jar spaghetti sauce

Cook shells according to package directions, drain and set aside. Mix cheeses, egg, parsley and oregano. Spoon cheese mixture into shells. Place stuffed shells into a 9x13 baking dish sprayed with cooking oil. Cover with spaghetti sauce and bake at 350 degrees for 25 to 30 minutes until heated through.

OKAY, I CONFESS... I'VE CHEATED. I'M NOT A NATURAL IN THE KITCHEN-I CAN'T JUST "WHIP" SOMETHING UP OUT OF WHAT'S IN THE PANTRY. I NEED TO WORK FROM A RECIPE. WELL THAT'S WHEN I MET PASTA-RONI. BOIL, DRAIN... SOUNDED LIKE AN EASY RECIPE. MUCH TO MY SURPRISE, THE ANGEL HAIR PASTARONI WAS ENJOYED BY ALL. I KEEP A STOCK ON HAND FOR THOSE "TOUGH NIGHTS" AND OFTEN TOSS IT WITH A BIT OF BROCCOLI OR HAM, AND ,SERVE WITH WARM BREAD.

Time Out Tuna Casserole

Makes 4 servings

4 cups egg noodles ,cooked
1 (8 oz.) package frozen mixed vegetables
2 (6 oz.) cans tuna
1 can cream of celery soup

Combine veggies, tuna and celery soup in a skillet. Cook over medium low heat until bubbly, stirring constantly. Stir in cooked egg noodles and simmer until heated through. Serve with Bedazzling Breadsticks.

(Personally, I don't really like tuna. However, my husband lives for the stuff. So to me—the perfect tuna recipe is one that he can easily make himself!)

> IF PASTA IS A FAVORITE FAMILY DISH, MAKE YOUR PANTRY PASTA-FRIENDLY BY KEEPING A FEW ITEMS ON-HAND AT ALL TIMES. MAKE SURE YOU HAVE A STOCK OF SPAGHETTI SAUCES, PARMESAN CHEESE, CANNED TOMATOES, TOMATO PASTE, FROZEN PEAS, CANNED MUSHROOMS, PESTO, BACON OR HAM, PREPARED ALFREDO SAUCE- KEEPING THOSE ITEMS ON DECK WILL ENSURE THERE IS ALWAYS SOMETHING TASTY FOR DINNER.

Late from Work Lasagna

Makes 8 servings

1 package lasagna noodles
1 (8 oz.) package ricotta cheese
1 (16 oz.) pkg. mozzarella cheese, divided
½ cup Parmesan cheese
1 egg
1 tablespoon chopped parsley
½ tablespoon oregano
1 pound ground beef
1 tablespoon minced garlic
1 large jar spaghetti sauce

Preheat oven to 375 degrees. Prepare lasagna noodles till soft but not cooked all the way through. Mix ricotta cheese ,1 cup (¼ package) of mozzarella cheese, ¼ cup Parmesan cheese, egg and parsley, set aside. Cook ground beef until crumbly and add oregano, garlic and spaghetti sauce to cooked ground beef. Put ½ cup of meat sauce on bottom of 9 x 13 inch baking dish. Place four cooked noodles on top of sauce and spread with ⅓ cheese mixture. Sprinkle this layer with 1 cup mozzarella cheese. Top this with 1 cup of meat mixture. Layer the rest of the ingredients in same order, reserving two cups of mozzarella cheese for the topping. Bake for 45-50 minutes.

"Multi-task" While this is baking, do the laundry, help the kids with their homework, walk the dog. This dish may be assembled the day before and refrigerated. Add 10-15 minutes to baking time. When preparing a lasagna for dinner, pick up some serving size aluminum trays from your local grocer before hand and make a few extra mini-lasagnas to freeze and use for quick meals.

Consider making several "flavors". Try a kid's version that is basically noodles, meat and cheese and then try one aimed at the adult palette—with garlic, onions, mushrooms, spinach and whatever else your heart desires.

Light & Easy Pasta Toss

16 ounces linguine
½ cup margarine
3 tablespoons fresh parsley, chopped
⅛ cup Dijon mustard
2 tablespoons lemon juice
3 cloves garlic, minced
salt and pepper to taste

Prepare pasta according to package directions. Melt butter in a pan over medium heat. Add parsley, mustard, lemon juice and garlic. Heat for 2-3 minutes. Toss sauce with pasta and then salt and pepper to
taste.

Spaghetti-o-no Its Dinner Time

Makes 4 servings

2 cans Spaghetti-o's™
1 pound ground beef
1 can corn, drained
1 can Italian tomatoes
1 can chili beans (optional)

Brown ground beef in large skillet. Add remaining ingredients (do not drain chili beans) and simmer for 15-20 minutes. This is a kid pleaser and a mom friendly dish. Nothing fancy but you feel like you cooked instead of just turning on the microwave.

PRESTO PASTA

Italian Pasta Skillet

3 packages of ramen noodles, beef flavor
1 pound ground round
20 oz. diced tomatoes, undrained
1½ cups water
1½ cups mozzarella cheese, shredded

Brown beef over medium heat. Drain. Add tomatoes, water and one seasoning packet of ramen and heat to boiling. Mix in noodles. Cook 5 minutes or until noodles are tender. Scoop onto plates and top with cheese.

Almost Oriental Noodle Dish

Makes 4 servings

1 pound beef boneless sirloin, cut into strips
1 can (14.5 oz) beef broth
¼ cup teriyaki sauce
2 cups rice noodles
1½ cups pea pods, if desired

Cook beef in a skillet over medium high heat for 4 minutes or until brown. Mix broth, teriyaki sauce and pea pods in skillet. Add noodles. Cook over medium heat for three minutes or until noodles are tender. Return beef to skillet and cook for an additional 2-3 minutes or until sauce thickens slightly.

USELESS TRIVIA

IT IS THOUGHT BY MANY THAT MARCO POLO INTRODUCED PASTA TO ITALY FOLLOWING HIS EXPLORATION OF THE FAR EAST IN THE LATE 13TH CENTURY.

Chicken and Ravioli

Makes 4 servings

1 pound pre-cooked chicken breast strips
   (such as Louis Rich™)
¾ cup chicken broth
9 oz. refrigerated ravioli
tad of Parmesan

Place broth and ravioli in skillet and heat to boiling. Cover and reduce heat, simmering for 3-5 minutes or until tender. Add chicken and heat through. Serve onto plates and top with a sprinkling of Parmesan cheese.

Parmesan Rotini

3 cups rotini pasta, uncooked
10 oz. frozen chopped broccoli
6 oz. pre-cooked chicken breast strips
2 tablespoons olive oil
½ cup Parmesan Cheese, grated
1 tomato, cut into bite-size pieces

Cook rotini according to package directions and drain. Steam broccoli. Add broccoli, chicken, Parmesan and tomato pieces to pasta and cook on low setting for a few minutes more, tossing together well.

USELESS TRIVIA

BY FEDERAL LAW, A NOODLE MUST CONTAIN 5.5 PERCENT EGG SOLIDS BY WEIGHT TO BE CALLED A NOODLE.

PRESTO PASTA

Magnificent Mac

3 cups chicken broth
1½ cups skim milk
¾ pound elbow macaroni
1½ tablespoons cornstarch
1½ cup frozen peas
½ pound Canadian bacon, cubed
8 oz. cheddar cheese, shredded

In a large sauce pan or Dutch oven bring broth, milk and macaroni to a boil. Cook for 10 minutes, stirring frequently. Blend cornstarch with 5 tablespoons of water. Stir into pan and continue stirring until mixture returns to a boil and begins to thicken. Add peas and bacon; mix well and then remove from heat. Add cheese and stir for 1-2 more minutes to melt.

Chicken Noodle Casserole

Makes 8 servings

16 oz. egg noodles, uncooked
1 cup non-fat sour cream
2 cups low-sodium chicken broth
¼ cup grated Parmesan cheese, divided
1 cup egg substitute
4 tablespoons Dijon mustard
3 cups chopped broccoli, blanched and drained
3 cups skinless, boneless chicken breast, cooked
¼ cup bread crumbs

Prepare egg noodles according to package directions; drain. Whisk the sour cream, chicken broth, half of the Parmesan cheese, eggs and mustard in a bowl until blended. Add noodles, broccoli and chicken and toss well. Transfer the mixture to a 9 x 12-inch baking dish.
Stir the remaining Parmesan and bread crumbs in a small bowl and sprinkle over casserole. Bake uncovered until bubbling around the edges and the top is golden brown, about 30-35 minutes. minutes. Let stand 5 minutes before serving.

A Sweet & Happy Ending...

Delectable Desserts

Quick Recipe Index:

Cinnamon Donuts in a Jiffy   48
Strawberry Sundaes   48
Tear-It-Up Tiramisu   49

Cinnamon Donuts in a Jiffy
Makes 10 servings

1 can refrigerated buttermilk biscuits (not the flaky kind)
Cinnamon sugar

Cut "donut holes" out of biscuits by using a 1 inch biscuit cutter. Heat oil in fryer. Fry 2 to 3 "donuts" at a time till brown, turning once. Fry "donut holes" separately. Drain on paper towels and immediately roll in cinnamon sugar and serve.

Strawberry Sundaes
Makes 4 servings

3 cups sliced strawberries
½ cup sugar
1 quart vanilla custard
Cool Whip® or whipped cream

Slice strawberries and mix with ½ cup sugar in covered container. Refrigerate for one hour to allow the strawberry sauce to form. Place 2 scoops vanilla custard in a serving dish and top with strawberry mixture. Top with whipped cream. (Since pasta dishes are so heavy, this is a good light ending to the perfect dinner. Note: best during strawberry season when fresh berries are at their prime.)

More Useless Trivia
GET YOUR FILL OF NOODLES DURING MARCH... NATIONAL NOODLE MONTH. HOWEVER... DO NOT CONFUSE NATIONAL NOODLE MONTH WITH NATIONAL PASTA MONTH, WHICH CELEBRATES ITSELF IN OCTOBER. (TRY USING YOUR NOODLE TO FIGURE THAT ONE OUT!)

Tear- It-Up Tiramisu

Makes 8 servings

1 (8 oz.) pkg. cream cheese, softened
½ cup strong coffee
2(1 oz.) squares semisweet chocolate, grated
1(12 oz.) container Cool Whip™
1 angel food cake
Chocolate syrup or hot fudge sauce

Beat cream cheese until fluffy—stir in ¼ cup coffee and grated chocolate, reserving 1 tablespoon of chocolate for garnish. Tear cake into 1 inch squares and place in 9 x 13 pan. Pour ¼ of remaining coffee over cake. Drizzle on chocolate syrup or hot fudge sauce in and stir to coat. Mix Cool Whip® with the cream cheese mixture and spread over top of cake mixture. Chill for two hours. Right before serving, drizzle with more chocolate sauce and sprinkle remaining chocolate shavings on top of the desert. Serve and enjoy!

Note: This dish uses angel food cake which is lower in fat and calories (and is easier to find) than lady fingers. Also the Cool Whip™ won't be as rich as the traditional custard version, but will deliver a great flavor and its simplicity more than makes up for the difference.

Pasta Buffet

A pasta bar buffet is a great choice for a slumber party. Serve pasta of different sizes and shapes. You can even make different colored pasta by adding a few drops of food coloring to the water. If you're really brave, let kids experiment with colors and see how many pasta colors they can create! Next, add some red sauce and white sauce. Lastly, offer assorted cheeses.

Your Personal Shopper

As the former Queen of Non-Cooking Excuses, one of those I used most often was that I just didn't have enough time to get organized, plan and get everything from the store. To avoid the same excuse-ridden fate in your future, I am including Your Personal Shopper right in this cookbook. You have three different five-day menus to choose from. You'll find a grocery list for each of those meal plans as well.

Your Personal Shopping List # 1

Your Five-Day Menu:
1. Easy Cheese Pasta (24) served with Tear-It-Up Tiramisu (49)
2. Chicken Tetrazzani (33) served with Fresh Bruschetta (16)
3. Spaghetti Pie (28) served with Garlic Bread (15)
4. Time Out Tuna Casserole (41) served with Cinnamon Donuts in a Jiffy (48)
5. Skimpy Scampi (36) served with Minestrone in a Minute (18)

Meats
- ☐ 4 chicken breasts
- ☐ 2 lbs. peeled fresh shrimp

Produce
- ☐ 2 tomatoes
- ☐ 1 clove garlic
- ☐ 2 onions
- ☐ small bunch parsley
- ☐ 1 small zucchini

Dry and Canned Goods
- ☐ 2 lbs. small pasta
- ☐ 2 cans cream of chicken soup
- ☐ 1 can cream of mushroom soup
- ☐ 1 lb. spaghetti pasta
- ☐ 2 cans Italian-style stewed tomatoes
- ☐ 2 cans (6 oz.) tomato paste
- ☐ Small bag sugar
- ☐ 4 cups egg noodles
- ☐ 2 cans (6 oz.) tuna
- ☐ 1 can cream of celery soup

- ☐ small bag flour
- ☐ 16 oz. fettuccine noodles
- ☐ 1 can lima beans
- ☐ 2 cans of beef broth
- ☐ 1 can kidney beans

Dairy
- ☐ butter
- ☐ 1½ cup shredded Swiss cheese
- ☐ 1 cup Parmesan cheese
- ☐ 1 qt. milk
- ☐ 8 oz. cream cheese
- ☐ 1 cup sour cream
- ☐ 2 eggs
- ☐ 1 cup fat-free cottage cheese
- ☐ 2½ cups shredded cheddar cheese
- ☐ 1 (12 oz.) container Cool Whip™

Frozen
- ☐ 1 (8 oz.) pkg. mixed vegetables
- ☐ 1 lb. Italian veggies

Spice List
- ☐ diced minced onions
- ☐ parsley flakes
- ☐ basil
- ☐ Worcestershire sauce
- ☐ oregano
- ☐ thyme
- ☐ salt and pepper
- ☐ garlic powder
- ☐ cinnamon sugar
- ☐ minced garlic

Other Stuff
- ☐ ½ cup strong coffee
- ☐ 1 oz. squares semisweet chocolate

- ☐ 1 angel food cake
- ☐ chocolate syrup
- ☐ 2 loaves French bread
- ☐ olive oil
- ☐ vegetable oil
- ☐ 1 can refrigerated buttermilk biscuits (not the flaky kind)
- ☐ cooking wine

Add Your Own Items:

_____
_____
_____
_____
_____
_____
_____
_____
_____
_____
_____
_____
_____
_____
_____
_____
_____
_____
_____
_____

Your Personal Shopping List # 2

Your Five-Day Menu:
1. Chicken and Ravioli (45) serve with Tossed Italiano Saladio (15)
2. Bowtie Bonanza (38) serve with Pepper Pasta Salad (17)
3. Tantalizing Turkey Dijon (23) serve with Turkey Noodle Soup (14)
4. Awesomely Easy Alfredo (25) serve with Bedazzling Breadsticks (14)
5. Fettuccine a la Ham (27) serve with Strawberry Sundaes (48)

Meats
- ☐ 1 lb. chicken breast strips (such as Louis Rich™)
- ☐ turkey pepperoni
- ☐ ¼ lb. ham
- ☐ 4½ cups turkey
- ☐ 12 oz. ham

Produce
- ☐ 1 bunch Romaine lettuce
- ☐ 1 onion
- ☐ 2 green peppers
- ☐ 2 tomatoes
- ☐ 10 cherry tomatoes
- ☐ 1 red onion
- ☐ 1 yellow pepper
- ☐ 1 red pepper
- ☐ 2 cloves garlic
- ☐ small bag carrots
- ☐ celery
- ☐ 3 cups strawberries

Dry and Canned Goods
- ☐ 4 (8 oz.) cans chicken broth
- ☐ 2 cans black olives

- ☐ 2 cans mushrooms
- ☐ 4 cups bowtie pasta
- ☐ 12 oz. pkg. rotini pasta
- ☐ 1½ lbs. fettuccine
- ☐ 1 lb. wide noodles
- ☐ 18 oz. evaporated skim milk
- ☐ corn starch
- ☐ 2½ oz. jar sliced mushrooms

Dairy
- ☐ large bag Mozzarella cheese
- ☐ 1 (8 oz.) cream cheese
- ☐ milk
- ☐ small can Parmesan cheese
- ☐ margarine
- ☐ small half & half
- ☐ ½ cup shredded cheese
- ☐ 1 qt. vanilla custard
- ☐ 1 small Cool Whip™

Frozen
- ☐ 1 bag asparagus
- ☐ 1 bag peas

Spice List
- ☐ salt and pepper
- ☐ garlic powder
- ☐ Italian seasoning
- ☐ oregano
- ☐ onion powder
- ☐ lemon peel
- ☐ dry mustard

Other Stuff
- ☐ 9 oz. refrigerated ravioli
- ☐ Italian dressing
- ☐ Dijon style mustard
- ☐ 1 can refrigerated biscuits
- ☐ sesame seeds (optional)
- ☐ poppy seeds (optional)
- ☐ dried minced onions (optional)
- ☐ sugar

Add Your Own Items:

Your Personal Shopping List # 3

Your Five-Day Menu:
1. Almost Oriental Noodle Dish (44) followed by Strawberry Sundaes (48)
2. Parmesan Rotini (45) served with Chicken Noodle Zupa (19)
3. Hammy Noodles (24) served with Fresh Bruschetta(16)
4. Italian Pasta Skillet (44) served with Garlic Bread (15)
5. Chicken Parmesan (35) served with Bedazzling Breadsticks (14)

Meats
- ☐ 1 lb. beef boneless sirloin
- ☐ 4 skinless chicken breast
- ☐ 2 lb. chicken
- ☐ ¾ lb. ham
- ☐ 1 lb. ground round

Produce
- ☐ 1 qt. strawberries
- ☐ 12 oz. pea pods
- ☐ 3 tomatoes
- ☐ 2 onions
- ☐ celery
- ☐ carrots

Dry and Canned Goods
- ☐ 1 can beef broth
- ☐ 1 lb. rice noodles
- ☐ 2 lbs. rotini pasta
- ☐ 2 cans chicken broth
- ☐ 1½ lbs. egg noodles
- ☐ 1¼ lbs. linguine
- ☐ 1 jar spaghetti sauce
- ☐ 3 pkgs. Ramen™ noodles, beef flavor
- ☐ 1 (20 oz.) can diced tomatoes

Dairy
- ☐ 1 qt. vanilla custard
- ☐ 1 small Cool Whip™
- ☐ grated Parmesan cheese
- ☐ 12 oz. shredded cheese (you choose the type, Parmesan, mozzarella, Swiss or cheddar)
- ☐ small light cream
- ☐ 1½ lbs. mozzarella cheese
- ☐ butter or margarine

Frozen
- ☐ 10 oz. chopped broccoli
- ☐ 1 bag peas

Spice List
- ☐ teriyaki sauce
- ☐ parsley
- ☐ salt and pepper
- ☐ bay leaf
- ☐ minced garlic
- ☐ basil
- ☐ oregano
- ☐ garlic powder
- ☐ dried minced onion (optional)

Other Stuff
- ☐ sugar
- ☐ olive oil
- ☐ flour

- ☐ 2 loaves French bread
- ☐ cooking spray
- ☐ 1 can refrigerated biscuits
- ☐ sesame seeds (optional)
- ☐ poppy seeds (optional)

Add Your Own Items:

Looking for more tips, recipes, and useless trivia. . .

The Rush Hour Cook™ is online with a full-featured site that is sure to impress you and your mother. Check it out at:

www.rushhourcook.com